By the same author

HISTORY
The Normans in the South
The Kingdom in the Sun, 1120–94
Reissued in one volume:
The Normans in Sicily

A History of Venice: The Rise to Empire
A History of Venice: The Greatness and the Fall
Reissued in one volume:
A History of Venice

Byzantium: The Early Centuries
Byzantium: The Apogee
Byzantium: The Decline and Fall
A Short History of Byzantium

TRAVEL
Mount Athos (with Reresby Sitwell)
Sahara
A Taste for Travel: An Anthology
Venice: A Traveller's Companion

MISCELLANEOUS
The Architecture of Southern England
Fifty Years of Glyndebourne
The Twelve Days of Christmas
Shakespeare's Kings
Christmas Crackers, 1970–79
More Christmas Crackers, 1980–89

Still More Christmas Crackers

being ten commonplace
selections by

JOHN JULIUS NORWICH

1990–1999

VIKING

VIKING

Published by the Penguin Group
Penguin Books Ltd, 27 Wrights Lane, London w8 5tz, England
Penguin Putnam Inc., 375 Hudson Street, New York, New York 10014, USA
Penguin Books Australia Ltd, Ringwood, Victoria, Australia
Penguin Books Canada Ltd, 10 Alcorn Avenue, Toronto, Ontario, Canada m4v 3b2
Penguin Books India (P) Ltd, 11 Community Centre,
Panchsheel Park, New Delhi – 110 017, India
Penguin Books (NZ) Ltd, Cnr Rosedale and Airborne Roads,
Albany, Auckland, New Zealand
Penguin Books (South Africa) (Pty) Ltd, 5 Watkins Street,
Denver Ext 4, Johannesburg 2094, South Africa

Penguin Books Ltd, Registered Offices: Harmondsworth, Middlesex, England

First published in one volume 2000
1

Individual selections copyright © John Julius Norwich, 1990, 1991, 1992, 1993
1994, 1995, 1996, 1997, 1998, 1999
This collection and introduction copyright © John Julius Norwich, 2000
All rights reserved

The moral right of the author has been asserted

The acknowledgements on p.340 constitute an extension of this copyright page

Set in 10/12pt Monotype Dante
Typeset by Rowland Phototypesetting Ltd,
Bury St Edmunds, Suffolk
Printed in England by Clays Ltd, St Ives plc

A CIP catalogue record for this book is available from the British Library

ISBN 0-670-89392-7

Contents

BOOK REVIEW
More Christmas Crackers, John Norwich, Penguin £9.99

Based on the selections of poetry and prose that Lord Norwich sends out each year to friends instead of Christmas cards, this anthology covers 1980–89 and includes contributions as diverse, but equally boring, as Virginia Woolf, Oscar Wilde, Edith Sitwell, Thomas Carlyle and Kingsley Amis. Covering subjects as important as pig-sticking, cooking puffins and Churchill's painting, it contains something to repel every taste. If Norwich is too mean to buy Christmas cards, why inflict extracts from his commonplace book on the public?

Scotland on Sunday
6 December 1992

Introduction

This is the third bound volume of my *Christmas Crackers*, and since I have written copious introductions to both its predecessors, there is little new to be said here. Indeed, if any readers of this book have any recollection of those previous essays, there is no need for them to plough through this. For the benefit of newcomers, however, I should explain that when I was living in Beirut in the late 1950s my mother gave me a beautiful album, bound in dark-blue Nigerian goatskin, which she intended to be used as a visitors' book. Unfortunately, within days of the volume's arrival, civil war broke out; the Lebanese Government declared a curfew and for several months thereafter we had no visitors at all. There was, on the other hand, plenty of time for reading; and the little notebook in which I had been in the habit of noting down short passages that had, for one reason or another, caught my fancy was fast filling up. One evening, therefore, when I had nothing better to do, I decided to copy them all into my still virgin album.

Then something remarkable happened. Instead of a heterogeneous pile of literary jottings, I suddenly realized that I had a proper commonplace book, something to be cultivated and nurtured and treasured, and to which the luxuriously tooled and gilded binding seemed to confer a wholly unexpected distinction. Some five years later that first album was full and I ordered another, in exactly the same format but this time in dark red. This was followed in due course by another, and another, with the colour changing each time; as I write these words I am about three-quarters of the way through Volume IX, which is bound in a particularly fetching shade of bottle green.

But commonplace collections, like every other kind, are no fun if they are not shared; and in the autumn of 1970 I deciced to have a little booklet printed containing a couple of dozen of my choicest items, and to send it round to my friends as a sort of glorified Christmas card. Production costs were modest in those days, and even these, I thought, might be recovered if I were to order a hundred or so extra copies and persuade one or two friendly booksellers to dispose of them as best they could.

The edition disappeared gratifyingly quickly, and so the following year I produced another – increasing my print order, in a burst of reckless optimism, from two hundred to three. That too sold out; and it was thus that the uncertain seedling became a moderately hardy annual, and I now find myself introducing the combined harvest of its third decade. Of these ten most recent numbers, only the front and back covers – which from 1990 onwards have carried designs instead of the previous single colour – have been omitted from the volume you now hold in your hands. As before, however, there are certain additions, in the shape of occasional afterthoughts of my own or pertinent observations by others. These I have put in square brackets. I have also once again included as a bonus, at the end of each year's offering, a twenty-fifth entry which, being over a page in length, could not be included in the ordinary *Cracker*.

In the first of my two previous introductions I listed what seemed to me the advantages of a commonplace collection such as mine. 'First of all,' I pointed out, 'it costs literally nothing, nicely bound volumes are useful for providing the initial impetus and for creating the sense of pride that every collector must develop to keep him going, but they are in no way essential. Secondly, being totally divorced from monetary wealth, it knows no restrictions of size or scope, accepting only those limitations which the collector himself decides to impose; it follows that no other form of collection can so fully reflect his taste and personality. Thirdly, he is on his own, far away from the world of catalogues and sale-rooms, experts and dealers. Indeed, one of the first lessons he learns is never to go out looking for anything; he is very unlikely to find it if he does, and the very act of searching seems in some curious way to blunten the antennae. If he can only keep these sharp, there is no telling where and when he will make his next *trouvaille*. He may not even need to wait until he next picks up a book; a chance remark, a letter from a friend, an opera programme, an advertisement, the instruction book for a new washing machine, a visit to a country church, a notice in a hotel room or railway station – any of these things, or a thousand others, can reveal the unexpected nugget of pure gold.'

All this is as true as it ever was; but for me there is, nowadays, yet another source, and a highly important one at that. As the *Crackers* have become better known, I have begun to receive superb contributions not only from old friends but from many people whom I have never met. (Some of these have now become friends too, in their own right.) This has, admittedly, one disadvantage: whereas in the early numbers virtually all the items I included were of my own finding, in recent years anything up to half the contents of any one *Cracker* may have come, as it were, from elsewhere. Still, the consequent dent in my self-esteem is probably no bad thing, and is anyway negligible when compared with the pleasure at seeing my collection enriched with new and wondrous treasures that I would never otherwise have encountered.

When these treasures have appeared in a subsequent *Cracker*, I have always tried to give proper acknowledgement of their sources; but I am conscious of having failed, all too often, to do so. In those instances where the omission was the result of a simple oversight, I have seized the present opportunity to repair it; but there are I fear a number of others where, in my excitement at the gift, I somehow forgot to record the name of the giver. To any benefactors still unacknowledged I can only apologize, assuring them that my apparent ingratitude is due to sheer absent-mindedness, and not to any desire to pass off their serendipity as my own.

To those who have sent me contributions that I have not yet used, let me again emphasize that the annual *Cracker* is not, and never has been, composed of pieces collected during the previous twelve months; it is a selection made, normally in the course of a February weekend, from the entire corpus of the past forty years. One or two items may indeed have been waiting almost as long before finally emerging in print. The mix is everything. The grave must lie down with the gay, the poetry with the prose, the cynical with the sad; and it is not always easy to make them do so.

Inevitably, however, there remains plenty of marvellous material – much of it of my own finding – which, though occupying a proud place in one or other of those nine albums, will never find its way into a *Cracker*. Sometimes it is simply unsuitable; more often I can offer no explanation except to say that, just as novelists or playwrights frequently find their characters to be assuming individual personalities that were never intended, so too the *Crackers*, in their modest way, seem to have developed an inner logic of their own. Some pieces fit; others, of equally high quality and every bit as welcome, obstinately refuse to settle down. I hope that when this happens their kind sponsors will understand, and will not be discouraged from keeping up the good work.

For this book is only a milestone; it is not the end of the road. Soon after its publication, the *Cracker* for the year 2000 will be on sale in all the usual bookshops – even, with any luck, in a few more. Whether this volume will be followed by another in ten years' time is anybody's guess; but I fully intend to go on until I drop, if only because I myself get far more fun out of it than anyone else does.

To all those who have sent me contributions, used or unused, over the years, I am equally and eternally grateful. Once again I record the immeasurable debts I owe to Alison Henning, without whose encourage-ment the first *Cracker* might easily have been the last; to John Saumarez Smith of Heywood Hill, whose enthusiasm – to say nothing of his salesman-ship – is an annual tonic; to my secretary Marion Koenig, for the countless hours she spends on problems of production, distribution and finance; and to all those, friends and strangers alike, who buy their copies year after year and have thus somehow managed to keep the whole slightly dotty enterprise on the road for as long as they have.

John Julius Norwich
London, July 2000

A Christmas Cracker

1990

After the death of Mary Tudor in 1558, Philip II of Spain married Elizabeth, the fourteen-year-old daughter of Henry II of France. The Duke of Alba stood proxy for Philip at the ceremony, and also – more surprisingly – at the official consummation of the marriage the same night. The Venetian ambassador, Giovanni Michiel, reported the details to his government:

The Queen retired to bed, and after her there entered, by the light of many torches, the King her father in company with the Duke of Alba. That Duke, having one of his feet bare, lifted the coverlet of the Queen's bed on one side, and, having inserted his foot beneath the sheet, advanced it until it touched the naked flesh of the Queen; and in such manner the marriage was understood to have been consummated in the name of King Philip through the agency of a third person – that which was never afterwards to be understood by anyone.

> To make his condiment your poet begs
> The pounded yellow of two hard-boiled eggs;
> Two boiled potatoes, passed through kitchen sieve,
> Smoothness and softness to the salad give.
> Let onion atoms lurk within the bowl
> And, half-suspected, animate the whole.
> Of mordant mustard add a single spoon,
> Distrust the condiment that bites so soon;
> But deem it not, thou man of herbs, a fault
> To add a double quantity of salt;
> Four times the spoon with oil of Lucca crown,
> And twice with vinegar procured from town;
> And lastly o'er the flavour'd compound toss
> A magic *soupçon* of anchovy sauce.
> Oh, green and glorious! Oh, herbaceous treat!
> 'Twould tempt the dying anchorite to eat;
> Back to the world he'd turn his fleeting soul,
> And plunge his fingers in the salad-bowl!
> Serenely full, the epicure would say,
> 'Fate cannot harm me, I have dined today.'

And one by my father, more characteristically, for a cocktail:

> Rum, divine daughter of the sugar cane,
> Rum, staunch ally of those who sail the sea,
> Jamaican rum of rarest quality!
> One half of rum the goblet shall contain.
> Bring Andalusian oranges from Spain,
> And lemons from the groves of Sicily;
> Mingle their juices (proportions two to three)
> And sweeten all with Demeraran grain.
> Of Angosturan bitters just a hint,
> And, for the bold, of brandy just a spice,
> A leaf or two of incense-bearing mint,
> And any quantity of clinking ice:
> Then shake, then pour, then quaff, and never stint,
> Till life shall seem a dream of Paradise.

This sonnet won a New Statesman *Weekend Competition. I still possess the glass shaker on which he lavished his winnings, and on which the verse is inscribed.*

Snubs:

The 5th Earl of Dysart, to George III angling for an invitation to visit his house at Ham:

'Whenever my house becomes a public spectacle, His Majesty shall certainly have the first view.'

Talleyrand, to a young man boasting of his mother's beauty:

'C'était donc monsieur votre père qui n'était pas beau.'

Politesse:

Vincenzo Valdrati, or Valdré (1742–1814) was an Italian painter-architect who came to England in the 1770s and designed, *inter alia*, several of the state rooms at Stowe before settling in Ireland, where he became Architect to the Board of Works. From Howard Colvin's superb *Biographical Dictionary of British Architects* I learn that 'while at Stowe he attended a wedding in the neighbourhood and, when the bridegroom failed to appear, chivalrously offered himself as a substitute – and was accepted'.

My friend Taffy Lloyd in Johannesburg has sent me a cutting from the South African press – or, more precisely, the Rosebank/Killarney Gazette *of 13 November 1985:*

FINAL FLING FOR CULTURE CLUB

The final fling for 1985 of the Parkview Library Culture Club will take the form of a short, interesting talk, followed by a party. This enjoyable event will take place on November 27 at the library which is on the corner of Athlone and Tyrone avenues, Parkview. It starts at 7:30 p.m.

Lieutenant P. Louw of the South African Police will advise on home security whilst people are away on holiday. Thereafter, everyone will mingle at a coffee and dessert party.

Anyone who would like to attend is invited to do so – admission is free. For further details, telephone the Parkview Library at 646-3375.

I know of no poem, by any poet living or dead, in which deliberate dissonance is used to such shattering effect as in these lines by George Herbert:

DENIALL

When my devotions could not pierce
    Thy silent ears;
Then was my heart broken, as was my verse:
My breast was full of fears
    And disorder:

My bent thoughts, like a brittle blow
    Did flie asunder:
Each took his way; some would to pleasures go,
Some to the warres and thunder
    Of alarms.

As good to any where, they say,
    As to benumme
Both knees and heart, in crying night and day,
Come, come, my God, oh come,
    But no hearing.

O that thou shoudst give dust a tongue
    To crie to thee,
And then not heare it crying! all day long
My heart was in my knee
    But no hearing.

Therefore my soul lay out of sight,
    Untun'd, unstrung:
My feeble spirit, unable to look right,
Like a nipt blossome, hung
    Discontented.

O cheer and tune my heartless breast,
    Deferre no time;
That so thy favours, granting my request,
They and my minde may chime,
    And mend my ryme.

I have not received many abusive letters in my life – a fact which makes this one all the more precious to me. It was written in consequence of a radio programme in which, many years ago, I acted as narrator. The writer signed it with his full name, and gave his address.

Sir,

Your brief sketch of Lord Edward Fitzgerald on Sunday night, apart from being an almost total distortion of the truth, was grossly offensive.

I realize that your employment as token peer in residence at the BBC merely required you to promulgate the prejudiced ignorance of [the author], who, as a true child of this venial age, can find no other explanation for true altruism than stupidity. Nevertheless in associating yourself with her egregious and ill-researched opinions you have not only impugned your own honour but have also gratuitously damaged the memory of one of the brightest ornaments of that caste to which I presume the Coopers [my own family] still hopefully aspire.

In the more spacious days in which Lord Edward lived you would have been made to answer for your insults on the field of honour, although in my view you demeaned yourself to a degree that would make a horse-whipping more appropriate.

I suggest the BBC mount a full-length programme on the life of Lord Edward in recompense for last Sunday's slander. If it did nothing else, such a programme would bring some of you face to face with the realities of physical and moral courage as well as true integrity and selflessness; a revelatory adventure into the unknown for most of you, I have no doubt.

Yours faithfully . . .

Lord Edward (1763–98) was an early champion of Irish independence. He died in Newgate prison, of wounds received when resisting arrest. 'Moore, who once saw him in 1797, speaks of his peculiar dress, elastic gait, healthy complexion, and the soft expression given to his eyes by long, dark eyelashes.' (DNB)

Here is a description of another – but very different – Edward FitzGerald, the translator of The Rubaiyat of Omar Khayam. *It comes from Robert Bernard Martin's superb biography of Tennyson – to which, ten years ago, we awarded the Duff Cooper Prize.*

In reaction to the grandeur of his own family, he hated ostentation or any kind of snobbishness, and the manifestation of either would draw his gentle reproof. Once in later years when he and Tennyson had listened to a common acquaintance talking of his titled friends, Fitz picked up a candle to go to bed, then turned at the door and said to Tennyson, 'I knew a Lord once, but he's dead.' When they were both old men and FitzGerald had been hurt by Tennyson's neglect, the worst he could think of to say to him was that he lived in too grand a manner. Spedding called Fitz 'the Prince of Quietists', and said that 'Half the self-sacrifice, the self-denial, the moral resolution which he exercises to keep himself easy, would amply furnish forth a martyr or a missionary. His tranquillity is like a pirated copy of the peace of God.'

Professor Martin's more recent – and equally enjoyable – biography of FitzGerald himself records that:

Among the scrapbooks in the Christchurch Mansion Museum in Ipswich that FitzGerald assembled from his reading is one proving his lifelong love of crime, murder trials, and low life. (Not that his idea of criminals was conventional, for among others he included a picture of his distant relative, Lord Edward Fitzgerald, under which he wrote, 'Noodle'.)

In 1989 we awarded the Duff Cooper Memorial Prize to Ian Gibson for his biography of Federico García Lorca. Lorca was for me a new discovery; what was a particular joy was to find that his poems were, nearly all of them, quite easily comprehensible to those who, like myself, do not speak a word of Spanish. Indeed, they almost make me feel I do.

Cada canción	*Every song*
es un remanso	*is a stillness*
del amor	*of love*
Cada lucero	*Every star*
un remanso	*a stillness*
del tiempo	*of time*
un nudo	*a knot*
del tiempo	*of time*
Y cada suspiro	*And every sigh*
un remanso	*a stillness*
del grito	*of a scream*

Those marvellous lines of his on the foundations of Granada need no translation:

¿Habéis sentido
en la noche de estrellas perfumada,
algo mas doloroso que su triste gemido?
Todo reposa en vago encantamiento
en la plata fluida de la luna.

Edith Sitwell's reaction to Lorca was favourable, even enthusiastic – but predictably unlike other people's:

His poems have such an intoxication that when reading them, and for many, many hours after, days after, one feels like a bumble bee that has been for a whole afternoon in the heart of a tiger-lily flower. We once had a lily here that bore 208 flowers on one stalk: it was photographed naturally for all the gardening papers. The bees came from miles around and there were the most disgraceful Bacchanalian scenes: bees hardly able to find their way home. That is what I feel about Lorca . . .

My hopes retire; my wishes as before
Struggle to find their resting-place in vain:
The ebbing sea thus beats against the shore;
The shore repels it; it returns again.

Walter Savage Landor

A nice little story about Frank Lloyd Wright, culled from Tom Wolfe's From Bauhaus to Our House:

. . . Wright developed a phobia toward Le Corbusier. He turned down his one chance to meet him. He didn't want to have to shake his hand. As for Gropius, Wright always referred to him as 'Herr Gropius'. He didn't want to shake his hand, either. One day Wright made a surprise visit to a site in Racine, Wisconsin, where the first of his 'Usonian' houses, medium-priced versions of his Prairie School manor houses, was going up. Wright's red Lincoln Zephyr pulled up to the front. One of his apprentices, Edgar Tafel, was at the wheel, serving as chauffeur. Just then, a group of men emerged from the building. Among them was none other than Gropius himself, who had come to the University of Wisconsin to lecture and was anxious to see some of Wright's work. Gropius came over and put his face at the window and said, 'Mr Wright, it's a pleasure to meet you. I have always admired your work.' Wright did not so much as smile or raise his hand. He merely turned his head ever so slightly toward the face at the window and said out of the side of his mouth, 'Herr Gropius, you're a guest of the university here. I just want to tell you that they're as snobbish here as they are at Harvard, only they don't have a New England accent.' Whereupon he turned to Tafel and said, 'Well, we have to get on, Edgar!' And he settled back, and the red Zephyr sped off, leaving Gropius and entourage teetering on the edge of the kerb with sunbeams shining through their ears.

Wolfe attributes this story to Tafel himself, who tells it in his book Apprentice to Genius: Years with Frank Lloyd Wright.

Meeting Patrick Barrington, who died earlier this year, you would never have guessed that he was a superb light poet. Here is one of his best efforts:

Although I never pandered to cruelty or greed,
I set too high a standard entirely to succeed;
I'm not a vegetarian – I never felt inclined
To so inhumanitarian an attitude of mind.

I can't help feeling sorry for a radish;
I can't help feeling pity for a pea.
How a man can be so narrow with a vegetable marrow
Has always been a mystery to me.
I look on it as cowardly and caddish
To massacre a peanut in its shell;
My views may be mistaken, but I keep to eggs and bacon;
And, after all, I manage very well.

I hate to see the life of a tomato
Inhumanly and mercilessly wrecked;
I look upon a beetroot as a sensitive and sweet root
Deserving admiration and respect.
I hate to see an apple in a tart, oh!
Imprisoned like a felon in a cell.
Humanity, awaken! Oh, return to eggs and bacon!
And, after all, you'll manage very well.

I weep for all the metres of asparagus they grow
For the vegetable-eaters of sinister Soho.
In some later generation – dare I hope? – will be revealed
Rather more consideration for the lilies of the field.

My creed, which many look upon as crazy,
Was formulated many years ago;
I believe these souls of ours go to dwell in fruits and flowers
When their human life is finished here below.
A stockbroker may turn into a daisy,
A barrister become a heatherbell.
This faith of mine's unshaken; that is why I keep to bacon,
And, after all, I manage very well.

I like to think a plum may be a Plato
For anything that anyone can know;
I like to think an onion may contain the soul of Bunyan,

Or a lettuce be the dwelling of Defoe.
King Ptolemy may lurk in this potato,
This celery be Shakespeare – who can tell?
Oh, leave its spears unshaken: not on Shakespeare but on bacon
I'll live; and I shall manage very well.

Lord Barrington may *have been right about our ultimate destination; I suspect, however, that Viola Meynell came nearer the mark when she wrote:*

> The dust comes secretly day after day,
> Lies on my ledge and dulls the shining things.
> But O this dust that I shall drive away
>   Is flowers and kings
> Is Solomon's Temple, poets, Nineveh.

Joachim du Bellay on Venice, after she had lost her commercial empire to the Turks but was still doggedly hanging on to her glory:

> Il fait bon voir, Magny, ces coïons magnifiques,
> Leur superbe arsenal, leurs vaisseaux, leur abord,
> Leur Saint-Marc, leurs palais, leur Réalté, leur port,
> Leur change, leurs profits, leur banque et leurs trafiques;
> Mais ce que l'on doit le meilleur estimer,
> C'est quand ces vieux cocus vont épouser la mer,
> Dont ils sont les maris et le Turc l'adultère.

Les Regrets, Sonnet 133

There was a most unfortunate incident in 1958, when before a football match at Wembley between England and Italy – the first to be televised across the whole of Europe, and with Pope Pius XII among the viewers – one of the Guards' military bands inadvertently played the national anthem of the former Italian monarchy. When asked for an explanation, the bandmaster replied that he had simply played from the book he had always used: 'Anthems of the Nations: 1908'.

To avoid future similar mishaps, the Admiralty asked the Foreign Office to provide the current texts and scores of the anthems of all the countries they were likely to visit. The following reply was sent from H.M. Consul-General, Muscat, to the Foreign Secretary, Lord Home:

British Consulate-General

Muscat

27 August, 1960

My Lord,

I have the honour to refer to Your Lordship's despatch No. 8 of July 29, in which you requested me to ascertain, on behalf of the Lords Commissioners of the Admiralty, whether the B flat clarinet music, enclosed with your despatch, was a correct and up-to-date rendering of the National Salute to the Sultan of Muscat and Oman.

2. I have encountered certain difficulties in fulfilling this request. The Sultanate has not since about 1937 possessed a band. None of the Sultan's subjects, so far as I am aware, can read music, which the majority of them regard as sinful. The Manager of the British Bank of the Middle East, who can, does not possess a clarinet. Even if he did, the dignitary who in the absence of the Sultan is the recipient of ceremonial honours, and who might be presumed to recognize the tune, is somewhat deaf.

3. Fortunately I have been able to obtain, and now enclose, a gramophone record which has on one side a rendering by a British military band of the 'Salutation and March to His Highness the Sultan of Muscat and Oman'. The first part of this tune, which was composed by the bandmaster of a cruiser in about 1932, bears a close resemblance to a pianoforte rendering by the Bank Manager of the clarinet music enclosed with Your Lordship's despatch. The only further testimony I can obtain of the correctness of this music is that it reminds a resident of long standing of a tune, once played by the long defunct band of the now disbanded Muscat infantry, and known at the time to non-commissioned members of His Majesty's forces as (I quote the vernacular) 'Gawd strike the Sultan blind'.

4. I am instructed by the Acting Minister for Foreign Affairs that there are now no occasions on which the 'Salutation' is officially played. The last occasion on which it is known to have been played at all was on a gramophone at an evening reception given by the Military Secretary in honour of the Sultan, who inadvertently sat on the record afterwards and broke it. I consider, however, that an occasion might arise when its playing might be appropriate: if, for example, the Sultan were to go aboard a cruiser which carried a band. I am proposing to call on His Highness shortly at Salalah on his return from London, and shall make further enquiries as to his wishes in the matter.

5. I am sending a copy of this despatch, without enclosures, to His Excellency the Political Resident at Bahrain.

I have, etc
J. F. S. Phillips.

Another friend, Forbes Taylor, writes to me that the present Sultan . . . 'maintains a number of bands, among them the Pipe variety who are required to perform Gilbert and Sullivan. The result is rather curious, as are the attempts of the Sultan's Royal Guard to march to 'Three Little Girls from School Are We' . . .

The poet Wilfred Owen was killed in battle early in the morning of 4 November 1918 – just a week before the Armistice. On Armistice Day itself his brother Harold was serving in HMS Astraea. *He writes in his book,* Journey from Obscurity:

We were lying off Victoria. I had gone down to my cabin thinking to write some letters. I drew aside the door curtain and stepped inside and to my amazement I saw Wilfred sitting in my chair. I felt shock run through me with appalling force and with it I could feel the blood draining away from my face. I did not rush towards him but walked jerkily into the cabin – all my limbs stiff and slow to respond. I did not sit down but looking at him I spoke quietly: 'Wilfred, how did you get here?' He did not rise and I saw that he was involuntarily immobile, but his eyes which had never left mine were alive with the familiar look of trying to make me understand; when I spoke his whole face broke into his sweetest and most endearing dark smile. I felt no fear – I had not when I first drew my door curtain and saw him there; only exquisite mental pleasure at thus beholding him. All I was conscious of was a sensation of enormous shock and profound astonishment that he should be here in my cabin. I spoke again. 'Wilfred dear, how can you be here, it's just not possible . . .' But still he did not speak but only smiled his most gentle smile. This not speaking did not now as it had done at first seem strange or even unnatural; it was not only in some inexplicable way perfectly natural but radiated a quality which made his presence with me undeniably right and in no way out of the ordinary. I loved having him there; I could not, and did not want to try to understand how he had got there. I was content to accept him, that he was here with me was sufficient. I could not question anything, the meeting in itself was complete and strangely perfect. He was in uniform and I remember thinking how out of place the khaki looked amongst the cabin furnishings. With this thought I must have turned my eyes away from him; when I looked back my cabin chair was empty . . .

I felt the blood run slowly back to my face and looseness into my limbs and with these an overpowering sense of emptiness and absolute loss . . . I wondered if I had been dreaming but looking down I saw that I was still standing. Suddenly I felt terribly tired and moving to my bunk I lay down; instantly I went into a deep oblivious sleep. When I woke up I knew with absolute certainty that Wilfred was dead.

The inscription by Thomas Carew on the tomb of Lady Mary Wentworth:

Good to the poor, to kindred dear,
To servants kind, to friendship clear,
To nothing but herself severe;

So, though a virgin, yet a bride
To every grace, she justified
A chaste polygamy, and died.

To my friend Richard Stilgoe I owe this English-language – if you can call it that – prospectus of the Storici Sbandieratori delle Contrade di Cori:

TEAM'S INTRODUCTION

The Folk International team of the 'HISTORIANS DISPLAYERS OF BANNERS OF CORI'S STREETS', organically formed by: the Ensign, the Trumpeters, and Drummer and the Displayers of Banners; are know famous because they tock plece in many International Manifestation.

She gets her origin from the Historian Carousel, old manifestation mistic-scenographic, remounting to the XVIo century which also today, periodically finds her natural development in the old CORI, City situated in the middle of Lazio 40 km. from ROME and preserves also now some medioevals manners of a high historian value.

The team, with his gorgeous costumes, the sounds, the wonderfull and fanciful plays to whom the displayers of banners know to give life, recreate as quick as lightning, popular atmosphere of times far and unknow. The high and limpid sound and the drummers roll gloomy and with rhythm, does together a natural background, accompanying and guiding them, to the banners which, commandet with ability by the displayers, swift, proud, exact, they draw, and create ancients figurations highly suggestives and show.

This becomes, in the roads trains, in the places and on the stages a show of colour, of force, of cleverness, which surprises tortures and exalt the spectator until he explodes at the end of the show in a natural, clamorous and unqualified approbation.

In the first-ever Cracker – of 1970 – I quoted those magical lines from Lycidas:

> So sinks the daystar in the Ocean bed,
> And yet anon repairs his drooping head,
> And tricks his beams, and with new sprangled Ore,
> Flames in the forehead of the morning sky.

and compared them with Victor Hugo's:

> Dans la nuit orageuse ou la nuit étoilée,
> Sa chevelure, aux crins de comètes mêlée,
>   Flamboie au front du ciel . . .

I have now found a third example of the same metaphor – or very nearly – in Canto XII of the Purgatorio:

> A noi venia la creatura bella,
> Bianco vestita, e nella faccia quale
> Par tremolando mattutina stella.

Mrs Ramsay translated it:

> Then came that lovely being from afar,
> Clothed in white robes, and bearing on his brow
> The trembling glory of the morning star.

In this instance, admittedly, the brow concerned is that of an angel rather than of the sky itself; but there is the same conjunction of ideas.

Dante loved that word tremolare; *from the* Purgatorio *again:*

> L'alba vinceva l'ora mattutina
> Che fuggia innanzi sì che di lontano
> Conobbi il tremolar della marina.

Pace *Mrs Ramsay:*

> The dawn was conquering the mists that flee
> Before it, as the early shadows wane;
> Afar I knew the trembling of the sea.

On 8 November 1956 George Lyttelton wrote to Rupert Hart-Davis:

I like the little interchange between old [James] Agate and [Lord Alfred] Douglas. J. A. wrote: 'Milton's poetry flames in the forehead of the morning sky. Housman's twinkles in the Shropshire gloaming; yours, my dear A., glitters like Cartier's window at lunch-time.' To which A. D. replied: 'Are you not aware that seventeen of my best sonnets were written in Wormwood Scrubs?'

I stopped believing in Santa Claus when I was six. Mother took me to see him in a department store and he asked for my autograph.

Shirley Temple

One of my favourite anthologies is Lord David Cecil's Library Looking-Glass –
not least for his commentaries on the chosen items. Here are three of them:

Words learnt through the ear, for some reason unknown to me, stir a
stronger imaginative and sensual response than words learnt through
the eye. Children, before they learn to read, enjoy the sound and flavour
of words as they seldom do later. Elizabethan literature shows a zest for
language now lost; and, to most Elizabethans, language was something
spoken rather than something written. It is a sad and bewildering truth
that literary style has got worse since everyone has learned to read.

Beauty as a critical term has been so overworked and misused that
critics hesitate to employ it. None the less, it is an indispensable term;
for it alone describes something that appeals at once to the imagination
and to the senses. It would be incorrect to call a well-cooked steak
beautiful; it appeals to the senses and not to the imagination. An
unselfish act on the other hand appeals to the imagination but not to
the senses; only metaphorically can it be called beautiful. But a rose
tree or a melody of Mozart are rightly called beautiful because they
appeal to both senses and imagination.

There is a provinciality in time as well as in space. To feel ill-at-ease
and out of place except in one's own period is to be a provincial in time.
But he who has learned to look at life through the eyes of Chaucer, of
Donne, of Pope and of Thomas Hardy is freed from this limitation. He
has become a cosmopolitan of the ages, and can regard his own period
with the detachment which is a necessary foundation of wisdom.

Some years ago my friend Ian Skidmore lent me a remarkable collection of pamphlets bound into a volume entitled Intemperance and Tight Lacing, Considered in Relation to the Laws of Life, *by one O. S. Fowler, Editor of the* American Phrenological Journal. *It was published in London in 1849, and the title-page carries the epigraph* Total Abstinence, or No Husbands – Natural Waists, or No Wives. *After seven closely written pages on the evils of corseting, Mr Fowler gets into his stride:*

Who does not know that the compression of any part produces *inflammation*? Who does not know that, *therefore*, tight-lacing around the waist keeps the blood *from* returning freely to the heart, and *retains* it in the bowels and neighbouring organs, and thereby *inflames all the organs of the abdomen*, which thereby EXCITES AMATIVE DESIRES? Away goes this book into the fire! 'Shame! Shame on the man who writes this!' exclaims Miss Fastidious Small-Waist. 'The man who wrote that, ought to be tarred and feathered!' Granted; and then what shall be done to the *woman* who *laces tight*? If it be improper for a man to *allude* to this *effort* of lacing, what is it for a *woman* to *cause* and *experience* it? . . .

To every man who prefers burying his children to the trouble or expense of raising them, I say, *marry a small waist*, and you will be sure to have few mature offspring, and those few thinned out by death . . . These infanticides, *with their corsets actually on*, are admitted into the sanctuary of the Most High God, and even to the communion-table of the saints!

Another pamphlet in the same volume is entitled Amativeness: or, Evils and Remedies of Excessive and Perverted Sexuality. *In the section on 'Matrimonial Excess' we read:*

But what stamps effectually the seal of nature's reprobation on excessive matrimonial indulgence, is its *destruction of the health of woman*. Is it not a most prolific cause of those distressing female complaints which *bury half our married women prematurely*, and seriously impair most of the remainder? . . . Speak out, ye weakly, nervous wives, now dying by wretched inches of these diseases, and say whether your sufferings were not caused mainly, and have not been aggravated to their present painfulness, by the frequency, the fury, the almost *goatishness*, of your husbands' demands? Reader, if thou knowest none such, thou knowest not the *cause* of all the deaths that transpire around thee!

From the diary of the Rev. Benjamin Newton, 1 September, 1816:

An entertaining German dined here who teaches the girls music and plays delightfully and sings well with no voice having been shot through the lung. A Mr Causer having been bit in a drunken frolic by a man of the name of Shipley in the leg last week is obliged to suffer amputation. During an armistice in which the Prussian and French officers were drinking together a son of Blücher gave for a toast the King of Prussia, which a French officer would not drink and soon after when it came to his turn gave Buonaparte which young Blücher would not drink, on which the officer went up to him and without saying anything struck him a smash in the face. Blücher said nothing but went out of the room and returned immediately with a pair of pistols, with one of which without uttering a word he shot the officer dead and then held up the other and said he had that ready for any man who would take up the quarrel. This came to his father's knowledge who put him under arrest for six weeks. Rode to Bewdley, no corn cut. Wrote to J. Fendall and received letters from Ward and his son. NB Dinner eaten entirely up.

She never found comfort
When a friend told her
To weep her pain away
And offered a shoulder.

But a thin tan lizard
Lying on a boulder,
Indifferent and delicate,
Greatly consoled her.

Marie de L. Welch

Bonus

In 1976 we awarded the Duff Cooper Prize to Mussolini's Roman Empire, *by Denis Mack Smith. Here is an extract:*

Mussolini still knew very little about Britain or America or the other English-speaking countries. His attitude to the British was based on a few platitudes and generalities: as he pronounced in 1935, they had not progressed since the Edwardian age and so had nothing to teach him. He had a 'mathematical certainty' that neither Britain nor France would ever declare war on Italy, because of their decline in population, and they could therefore be provoked with impunity. Early in 1936 he asked the director general of statistics to work out details of this decline, and then announced that, since 11 million people in Britain were over fifty years old, here was proof positive that they would never fight another war. The fact that there were 2 million more British women than men told in the same direction, and he calculated that there would soon be only 30 million people in the British Isles, 'all of them very old': here, he explained, was a fact of fundamental significance. Taking it into account alongside the figures for alcoholism and sexual perversion, fascism could safely assume that Britain was finished and her Empire about to disintegrate.

Whenever it became clear which way Mussolini's mind was working, the journalists and place-hunters competed to reinforce his arguments, and this particular topic is a good example of how far propaganda could be exaggerated as political differences with London became more acute. One expert announced that there were 7 million spinsters in Britain because they were too ugly to get married; another view was that the British population would soon be down to 20 millions or would even disappear entirely in a few decades, unless the monarch intervened and permitted polygamy. Medical specialists gave it as their opinion that the practice of birth control was chiefly to blame because it caused sterility among English women, and Dr Cucco, a specialist from Palermo and one-time member of the Fascist Grand Council, found from his researches that contraception also led to conjunctivitis, nervous asthma, dyspepsia, bad memory, insomnia, excitability, and a ceaseless anxiousness and irritability: his learned thesis was favourably reviewed by the medical press, by the Vatican newspaper, and by the Royal Academy.

Another doctor thought that the fatal decrease in births among the British, like their notorious cowardice and unwillingness to fight, was due rather to the mutilating operation of tonsillectomy, and here too was another comfortable assurance that this decadent people was unlikely to hit back if attacked.

The fascist leaders did not have much experience of the outside world. Mussolini continued to think of the British as a people who put on evening dress when they took tea at five o'clock. Achille Starace, who after 1931 came second in the hierarchy, was unwilling to believe that Eire was a separate and possibly friendly country. But a half-knowledge of English literature was used by the professors to demonstrate that the British were no less decadent than the French. Virginia Woolf was evidence of loss of masculinity, Galsworthy's *Forsyte Saga* of narrow materialism, Chesterton and Belloc of the nation's drunkenness. The reading of Samuel Pepys was recommended by Guido Piovene so as to be able to understand the avarice, the social conformism, the sensual vulgarity which existed behind the mask of every Englishman. One student discovered the typical Englishman in Dr Jekyll and Mr Hyde, another found him in the Bertie Wooster of P. G. Wodehouse, who 'was not the invention of a novelist, but rather the ordinary type of Englishman as he has emerged from generations of repressed Victorians'.

The propagandists were anxious to correct certain historical misconceptions, among them those which had been invented by Gibbon and other similarly partisan writers. It was a misconception to say that there had ever been friendliness between Italy and England. Italy had not only rescued Britain and France from defeat in 1918, but was generally recognized to have surpassed them and become 'the first nation in the world'. With the aid of such authoritative texts as *1066 and All That*, an interesting picture was built up of Britain as an effete country corrupted by wealth and power, undermined by puritanism, ruined by the Jews and psychoanalysts, and by the national habit of eating five meals a day. In Scotland the aristocracy was said to maintain its feudal position by the help of private armies, while at the other extreme the British workman could not afford even one meal a day, and tens of thousands of people in London were dying of hunger each year.

A
Christmas
Cracker

1991

A few items from the published List of Wedding Presents to Princess Anne and Captain Mark Phillips, subsequently exhibited at St James's Palace:

Item No.

100.   TADEUSZ ROGALA
        Book, *Sewers of Warsaw*

179.   MRS E. E. GOTT
        Nine 2½p stamps

258.   PATTY McHUGH
        A literary publication

285.   MRS VALERIE ROGERS
        Novelty handcuffs

294.   MRS ANGELA KILMARTIN
        Book, *Understanding Cystitis*

300.   MRS MATILDA B. KAPICKA
        A packet of SQUASH seeds

499.   REV. CANON AND MRS C. L. CONDOR
        Three felt mice

545.   MR SEYFETTIN TUNC
        Book, *O World Stop Revolving*, by the donor

591.   MR F. PELLA
        Various carvings out of coal

795.   MRS B. R. SMITH
        Booklet, *Mothers of Kentucky*

1242.   MRS N. CLEARY
        Talcum powder

1247.   MRS M. E. COE
        Picture postcards of San Diego

1252.   DR AND MRS PATRICK HARDY
        Game, *Oops!*

Robert Ross, best known nowadays as the loyal friend of Oscar Wilde, reminisces about 'the educational works popular in my childhood':

In one of these books, general knowledge was imparted after the manner of Magnall: 'What is the world? – The earth on which we live.' 'Who was Raphael?' 'How is rice made?' After such desultory interrogatives, without any warning, came Question 15: 'Give the character of Prince Potemkin' –

'Sordidly mean, ostentatiously prodigal, filthily intemperate and affectedly refined. Disgustingly licentious and extravagantly super-stitious, a brute in appetite, vigorous though vacillating in action.'

I cannot like Tess of the d'Urbervilles; *Hardy seems to me to inflict so many miseries on his unfortunate heroine that one begins to suspect him of more than a touch of literary sadism. But when he forgets his disagreeable plot and starts thinking about his beloved Dorset countryside, how evocatively he can write:*

At these non-human hours they could get quite close to the water-fowl. Herons came, with a great bold noise as of opening doors and shutters, out of the boughs of a plantation which they frequented at the side of the mead; or, if already on the spot, hardily maintained their standing in the water as the pair walked by, watching them by moving their heads round in a slow, horizontal, passionless wheel, like the turn of puppets by clockwork.

They could then see the faint summer fogs in layers, woolly, level, and apparently no thicker than counterpanes, spread about the meadows in detached remnants of small extent. On the gray moisture of the grass were marks where the cows had lain through the night – dark-green islands of dry herbage the size of their carcases, in the general sea of dew. From each island proceeded a serpentine trail, by which the cow had rambled away to feed after getting up, at the end of which trail they found her; the snorting puff from her nostrils, when she recognized them, making an intenser little fog of her own amid the prevailing one. Then they drove the animals back to the barton, or sat down to milk them on the spot, as the case might require.

Or perhaps the summer fog was more general, and the meadows lay like a white sea, out of which the scattered trees rose like dangerous rocks. Birds would soar through it into the upper radiance, and hang on the wing sunning themselves, or alight on the wet rails subdividing the mead, which now shone like glass rods. Minute diamonds of moisture from the mist hung, too, upon Tess's eyelashes, and drops upon her hair, like seed pearls. When the day grew quite strong and commonplace these dried off her; moreover, Tess then lost her strange and ethereal beauty; her teeth, lips and eyes scintillated in the sunbeams, and she was again the dazzlingly fair dairymaid only, who had to hold her own against the other women of the world.

Regular Cracker readers will be aware of my fondness for the poet Samuel Daniel (1562–1619). Here is another sonnet of his:

When men shall find thy flower, thy glory, pass
    And thou with careful brow sitting alone
Receivèd hast this message from thy glass,
    That tells thee truth and says that all is gone,
Fresh shalt thou see in me the wounds thou madest,
    Though spent thy flame, in me the heat remaining;
I that have loved thee thus before thou fadest,
    My faith shall wax, when thou art in thy waning.

The world shall find this miracle in me,
    That fire can burn when all the matter's spent,
Then what my faith hath been thyself shall see,
    And that thou wast unkind thou may'st repent.
      Thou may'st repent that thou hast scorned my tears,
      When winter snows upon thy sable hairs.

A letter addressed in 1905 by the Indian stationmaster at Londiani, Kenya, to his senior officer in Nairobi:

Most Honoured and Respected Sir,

I have the honour to humbly and urgently require your Honour's permission to relieve me of my onerous duties at Londiani so as to enable me to visit the land of my nativity, to wit, India, forsooth.

This in order that I may take unto wife a damsel of many charms who has long been cherished in the heartbeats of my soul. She is of superfluous beauty and enamoured of the thought of becoming my wife. Said beauteous damsel has long been goal of my manly breast and now am fearful of other miscreant deposing me from her lofty affections. Delay in consummation may be ruination most damnable to romance of both damsel and your humble servant.

Therefore, I pray your Honour, allow me to hasten to India and contract marriage forthwith with said beauteous damsel. It is dead loneliness here without this charmer to solace my empty heart.

If, however, for reasons of State or other extreme urgency, the Presence cannot suitably comply with terms of this humble petition, then I pray your most excellent Superiority to grant me this benign favour for Jesus Christ's sake, a gentleman whom your Honour very much resembles.

I have the honour to be, Sir, your Honour's most humble and dutiful, but terribly love-sick, mortal withal.

[Signature]

B.A. (failed by God's misfortune)
Bombay, Bombay University, and
now station-master, Londiani.

The request was, we are told, granted.

39

Look back across the Tiber as the city spreads beneath our feet in all its mellow tints of white, and red, and brown, broken here and there by masses of dark green pine and cypress, and by shining cupolas raised to the sun. There it all lies beneath us, the heart of Europe, and the living chronicle of man's long march to civilization.

G. M. Trevelyan,
Garibaldi's Defence of
the Roman Republic

Hempsted House, in the village of Hempsted, Gloucestershire, was formerly the Rectory. It has a pretty doorway with strapwork in carved stone, on which are inscribed the words:

> Who'er doth dwell within the door
> Thank God for Viscount Scudamore

> 1671

Lord Scudamore, I learn from the Dictionary of National Biography, died in that year at the age of 70. From 1634 to 1638 he was Charles I's Ambassador in Paris. He conferred two major benefits on humanity: first, the restoration – at his own considerable expense – of the marvellous church of Abbeydore in Herefordshire; second, his development of the redstreak apple, described by the poet John Philips, in the course of his Miltonic epic on Cyder, as being

> Of no regard till Scudamore's skilful hand
> Improv'd her, and by courtly discipline
> Taught her the savage nature to forget
> Hence styled the Scudamorean plant.

The Hempsted inscription reminds me of another, said to have been carved on an obelisk standing on the road between Inverary and Inverness:

> If you'd seen these roads before they were made,
> You would hold up your hands and bless Marshal Wade.

Wade it was who was sent as Commander-in-Chief to Scotland to put down the Young Pretender in 1745. (There is a splendid bust of him by Roubiliac in the south aisle of Westminster Abbey.) His mission was unsuccessful – Prince Charlie gave him the slip – but his roads were so good that he was forgiven.

In his ever-enjoyable correspondence with Rupert Hart-Davis, George Lyttelton quotes the following triads, 'from inscriptions on the Great Wall of China':

The Three Good Things:

> Certainty held in Reserve
> Unexpected Praise from an Artist
> Discovery of Nobility in Oneself.

The Three Bad Things:

> Unworthiness Crowned
> Unconscious Infraction of the Laws of Behaviour
> Friendly Condescension of the Imperfectly Educated.

Rupert replies with:

The Three Rare Things (Sights of the Kingfisher):

> Clear Memory of Romantic Conversation
> The Meeting of Great Equals
> Unremarked Abbreviation of Pious Exercises.

The Three Foolish Things (Spring Lambs):

> Deep Sleep in an Unknown House
> Setting to Sea in a Borrowed Junk
> Not to Lag Behind when the Elephant approaches a New Bridge.

Elsewhere in the correspondence George quotes the following addition, 'which the late Geoffrey Madan claimed to have culled from Chinese literature':

The Three Illusions:

> To Think Investment Secure
> To Imagine that the Rich Regard you as their Equal
> To suppose your Virtues Common to All and your Vices
>   Peculiar to Yourself.

Mention of Geoffrey Madan produces an immediate resurgence of a temptation that I have always tried to resist: it is, I feel, a kind of cheating to raid the commonplace books of others. But Madan was in a class by himself, so I shall resist no longer. Here are a few of his jottings:

– Peel's smile: like the silver plate on a coffin.

– Duke of Wellington disapproved of soldiers cheering, as too nearly an expression of opinion.

– George III not having seen the sea aged 34 (H. Walpole memoirs).

– *Important if True*. Inscription which Kinglake wanted on all churches.

– A. See B. A correspondence between two clergymen on Baptism and Regeneration. 1825.
– ZZ. Genuine will of clergyman, lately deceased, whose son deservedly possesses one of the highest stations in the Church: containing his remarkable apology for adultery. 1750.

> (First and last entries in BM catalogue)

– Sights of London: the church in Leicester Square where Mme Navarro, between the matinée and the evening performances, used to pray to be delivered from the attentions of King Edward VII.

– Rhodes spending £8,000 on having translations made of all Gibbon's authorities.

– Mysterious frame, with ivory measuring-strip, in sub-basement of 148 Piccadilly [the Rothschilds' London house]. For measuring footmen: if one grew too fast, he could be exchanged for one from Tring.

– Mrs Yates Thompson told me that she crossed the Channel with Ruskin on a rough day: he recommended *jumping* as a cure for sea-sickness.

– The last dream of bliss: staying in heaven without God there.

And, talking of Ruskin, should not these words of his be inscribed above the door of every planning authority in the land?

A single villa can mar a landscape, and dethrone a dynasty of hills.

No student of architecture, certainly, should ever forget his invaluable advice:

Don't look at buildings: *watch* them.

My friend Tony Sutcliffe sends me an epitaph from Lydford, Devon:

Here lies, in horizontal position,
the outside case of
GEORGE ROUTLEIGH, Watchmaker;
Whose abilities in that line were an honour
to his profession.
Integrity was the Mainspring, and prudence the Regulator
Of all the actions of his life.
Humane, generous and liberal,
his Hand never stopped
till he had relieved distress.
So nicely regulated were all his motions,
that he never went wrong,
except when set a-going
by people
who did not know his Key;
Even then he was easily
set right again.
He had the art of disposing his time so well,
that his hours glided away
in one continual round
of pleasure and delight,
until an unlucky minute put a period
to his existence.
He departed this life,
Nov. 14, 1802,
aged 57:
wound up,
in hopes of being taken in hand
by his Maker;
and of being thoroughly cleaned, repaired,
and set a-going
in the world to come.

From Baedeker's Southern Italy, *on Baiae:*

Luxury and profligacy, however, soon took up their abode at Baiae, and the desolate ruins, which now alone encounter the eye, point the usual moral!

The preface to the same volume offers some sensible advice:

The traveller should adopt the Neapolitan custom of rejecting fish that are not quite fresh.

John Armstrong (1709–1779) was a doctor and a poet. In the former capacity, despite being appointed Physician to the Army in Germany in 1760, he enjoyed only limited success since, as he put it, 'he could neither tell a heap of lies in his own praise wherever he went; nor intrigue with nurses; nor associate, much less assimilate, with the various knots of pert insipid, lively stupid, well-bred impertinent, good-humoured malicious, obliging deceitful, waspy drivelling gossips; not enter into juntos with people who were not to his liking'. Among his literary works, his first venture into poetry, The Oeconomy of Love *of 1736, was published anonymously: 'indeed', as the* Dictionary of National Biography *somewhat cattily remarks, 'it is a production which not many men would care to claim'; his* Art of Preserving Health, *on the other hand, is said on its publication in 1744 to have achieved immediate popularity. Of a man of sound digestion the Doctor writes:*

> Nor does his gorge the luscious bacon rue,
> Nor that which Cestria sends, tenacious paste
> Of solid milk

– a substance which one takes a moment or two to identify as Cheshire cheese. He must also be the only medical writer to have suggested that the recitation of the ancient authors may be beneficial in the treatment of constipation:

> Read aloud resounding Homer's strain,
> And wield the thunder of Demosthenes;
> The chest so exercised improves its strength,
> And quick vibrations through the bowels drive
> The restless blood, which in inactive days
> Would loiter else in inelastic tubes.

The more I read about Rossini, the more I love him. At the end of the full manuscript score of his enchanting Petite Messe Solonelle – *a misnomer, if ever there was one – he has written, in French:*

Douze chanteurs et trois sexes: hommes, femmes et castrats, suffiront pour l'exécution, soit huit pour le choeur et quatre solistes, qui formeront en tout douze chérubins. Seigneur, pardonne-moi le rapprochement suivant. Il y a également douze apôtres dans le fameux coup de mâchoire que Léonard de Vinci a peint en fresque: la soi-disant Sainte-Cène. Qui le croirait? Il y a parmi Tes disciples certains qui chantent faux!! Seigneur, aie pitié: je T'assure qu'à mon déjeuner il n'y aura pas de Judas et que mes disciples chanteront Tes louanges correctement et avec amour dans cette petite composition qui est, j'en ai peur, le dernier péché mortel de ma vieillesse. Dieu Bon, la voici terminée, cette pauvre petite messe. Je ne sais pas si c'est de la musique sacrée ou de la sacrée musique. Je suis né pour l'opéra-bouffe, comme Tu le sais. Peu de science, un peu de coeur, et c'est tout. Donc, laisse-moi chanter Tes louanges et accorde-moi Ton Paradis. – G. Rossini – Paris 1863.

[*It might be translated like this:*

Twelve singers and three sexes – men, women and castrati – are all that is necessary for a performance: a choir of eight and four soloists, a dozen cherubim in all. Dear Lord, forgive me if I make a comparison: there are also twelve apostles in the famous conversation piece that Leonardo da Vinci turned into a fresco – the so-called Last Supper. Who'd have thought it? Among Your disciples there are some who sing out of tune! Have pity, Lord: I promise you that at my table there will be no Judases, and that my disciples will sing Your praises properly and with love in this little piece which is, I fear, the last mortal sin of my old age. Here it is, merciful Lord, this poor little mass. I don't know whether it is sacred music or damned music. I was born for comic opera, as You know. A little knowledge, a little heart, and that's all. So let me sing Your praises – and grant me Your paradise.

G. Rossini
Paris 1863

'Musique sacrée' and 'sacrée musique' – the pun is untranslatable; but I have been a good deal more worried by 'coup de mâchoire': even my French friends cannot agree on its meaning.]

A short verse on the subject of wine, by Gavin Ewart:

> A remarkable thing about wine
> Which we drunkards and lechers all bless so,
> Is the way it makes girls look more fine –
> But ourselves, on the contrary, less so.

And two on the Dry Martini. I do not know the author of the first:

> 'I like a Martini,' said Mabel,
> 'But I've learned to take two at the most;
> For with three I am under the table –
> After four, I am under my host.'

The second is a near-limerick by Ogden Nash:

> There is something about a Martini
> Ere the dining and dancing begin;
> And to tell you the truth,
> It's not the vermouth –
> I think that perhaps it's the gin.

Towards the end of 1988, The Times ran a correspondence on wanted and unwanted Christmas presents. By far the best letter was published on November 23 – remarkable, it seems to me, not only for the dreadful tale it has to tell but for the superb economy of its style. There is not a wasted word; and the impact of the last sentence is quietly shattering.

Sir,

The worst passed-on present my father ever received from his eldest sister was a pair of what looked like unused bedsocks. He, in fury, gave them to me.

When I put them on I found, to my horror, a used corn plaster in one of the toe ends. My aunt, at the time, kept a small private hotel.

Yours faithfully,

J. B. Prior

In 1854 the Government of the United States sought to buy a vast tract of land from one of the western Indian tribes. The Chief, whose name was Sealth, or Seattle, replied in a long oration known as Chief Seattle's Testimony. Here is an extract, kindly sent me by David Attenborough:

We are a part of the earth and it is part of us.
The perfumed flowers are our sisters;
The deer, the horse, the great eagle,
These are our brothers.
The rocky crests, the juices of the meadows,
The body heat of the pony, and man
– All belong to the same family.

So, when the Great Chief in Washington sends word
That he wishes to buy our land, he asks much of us . . .

We will consider your offer to buy our land.
If we decide to accept, I will make one condition:
The white man must treat the beasts of this land
As his brothers.

I am a savage and I do not understand any other way.
I have seen a thousand rotting buffalos on the prairie,
Left by the white man who shot them from a passing train.
I am a savage and I do not understand how the smoking
Iron horse can be more important than the buffalo
That we kill only to stay alive.

What is man without the beasts?
If the beasts were gone, man would die from a great
Loneliness of spirit. For whatever happens to the beasts
Soon happens to man. All things are connected.

This we know. The earth does not belong to man;
Man belongs to the earth.
This we know. All things are connected like the blood
Which unites one family.
All things are connected.

Whatever befalls the earth befalls the sons of the earth.
Man did not weave the web of life, he is merely a strand in it.
Whatever he does to the web, he does to himself.

The recent death of Malcolm Muggeridge reminded me of a long interview which he gave to the Sunday Times *on Easter Sunday 1981. He was talking about his parents, and in particular about their religious beliefs. In answer to the question 'Was your father devout?' he replied:*

'Not at all. But he saw Jesus as quite a good chap, as the honourable member for Galilee South.'

As for his mother:

'She was more religious and more working class. I once laughed at the story of Daniel in the Lions' Den and I'll always remember that she said "If *that's* not true, then nothing's true".'

An incident in Cairo, described by Sir Ronald Storrs in Orientations:

Some time in 1906 I was walking in the heat of the day through the bazaars. As I passed an Arab café an idle wit, in no hostility to my straw hat but desiring to shine before his friends, called out in Arabic, 'God curse your father, O Englishman.' I was young then and quicker tempered, and foolishly could not refrain from answering in his own language that I would also curse his father if he were in a position to inform me which of his mother's two and ninety admirers his father had been. I heard footsteps behind me and slightly picked up the pace, angry with myself for committing the sin Lord Cromer would not pardon – a row with Egyptians. In a few seconds I felt a hand on each arm. 'My brother,' said the original humorist, 'return, I pray you, and drink with us coffee and smoke.' (In Arabic one speaks of 'drinking' smoke.) 'I did not think that Your Worship knew Arabic, still less the correct Arabic abuse and we would fain benefit further by your important thoughts.'

My friend Michael Trinick contributes the following from The Spirit of the Public Journal *for 1825:*

The custom of conveying approbation or applause by *humming*, prevalent in the seventeenth century, is well illustrated by the following curious anecdote from Johnson's *Lives of the Poets*, 1809, vol. ii, p. 41:

> Bishop Burnet is not very favourable to the memory of Bishop Sprat; but he and Burnet were old rivals. On some public occasion, they both preached before the House of Commons. There prevailed in those days an indecent custom: when the preacher touched any favourite topic in a manner that delighted his audience, their approbation was expressed by a loud *hum*, continued in proportion to their zeal or pleasure. When Burnet preached, part of his congregation *hummed* so loudly, and so long, that he sat down to enjoy it, and rubbed his face with his handkerchief. When Sprat preached, he likewise was honoured with the same animating *hum*; but he stretched out his hands to the congregation, and cried, 'Peace, peace! I pray you peace!'

This custom was continued in the Universities in 1766, and perhaps later, as appears from the testimony of the Rev. Samuel Pegge, LL D, who, in a curious posthumous volume of observations intituled *Anonymiana*, p. 467, says, 'That way of giving applause by *humming*, now practised in our Universities (for which reason, in a *tripos* speech, they were once called *Hum et Hissimi Auditores*) is a method not unknown to barbarous nations.'

Dr Charles Burney, writing of his visit to Venice in 1770, notes that:

At the Hospitals and in Churches, where it is not allowed to applaud in the same manner as at the Opera, they cough, hem, and blow their noses to express admiration.

David Newsome's admirable biography of A. C. Benson, On the Edge of Paradise, *has furnished some valuable additions to my collection of stories about Henry James:*

> Passing him in the Athenaeum, Arthur [Benson] asked him whether he would give him his blessing. 'My dear Arthur,' Henry James replied, 'my mind is so constantly and continuously bent upon you in wonder and goodwill that any change in my attitude could only be the withholding of a perpetual and settled felicitation.'

> Asked by Gosse if any of a party of actresses who called with Ellen Terry to meet the great man struck him as being particularly pretty, 'H. J. turned up his eyes and held up his hands in speechless horror at the indelicacy of the suggestion. Then, after a long pause, he said "I must not go so far as to deny that one poor wanton had some species of cadaverous charm".'

From the Journal of Mrs Arbuthnot, 28 July 1821:

I went to the opera, where the Duke [of Wellington] came to me. We were admiring the ballet, and the Duke told me he would tell me a very *odd* story if I wd. promise not to be shocked or angry. He said that when Bonaparte came to Paris from Russia the whole town talked of nothing but the loss of the army and it was felt to be very desirable to give them some other topic of conversation. Bonaparte's expedient was to make the women dancers at the Opera dance *without their undergarment!* and actually sent an order to that effect! The women, however, positively refused; but did any one ever hear of such a proposal? Tho' the Duke said that, if the women had consented, he did not doubt but that it would have obliterated all recollection of the Russian losses, for in that country they have not the decency which, in this, wd. cause women so dressed to be hissed off at once. This anecdote he said he knew for a fact.

'How far is St Helena from a little child at play?'
What makes you want to wander there with all the world between?
Oh, Mother, call your son again or else he'll run away.
(*No one thinks of winter when the grass is green!*)

'How far is St Helena from a fight in Paris street?'
I haven't time to answer now – the men are falling fast.
The guns begin to thunder, and the drums begin to beat.
(*If you take the first step, you will take the last!*)

'How far is St Helena from the field of Austerlitz?'
You couldn't hear me if I told – so loud the cannon roar.
But not so far for people who are living by their wits.
(*'Gay go up' means 'gay go down' the wide world o'er!*)

'How far is St Helena from an Emperor of France?'
I cannot see – I cannot tell – the Crowns they dazzle so.
The Kings sit down to dinner, and the Queens stand up to dance.
(*After open weather you may look for snow!*)

'How far is St Helena from the Capes of Trafalgar?'
A longish way – a longish way – with ten year more to run.
It's South across the water underneath a falling star.
(*What you cannot finish you must leave undone!*)

'How far is St Helena from the Beresina ice?'
An ill way – a chill way – the ice begins to crack.
But not so far for gentlemen who never took advice.
(*When you can't go forward you must e'en come back!*)

'How far is St Helena from the field of Waterloo?'
A near way – a clear way – the ship will take you soon.
A pleasant place for gentlemen with little left to do.
(*Morning never tries you till the afternoon!*)

'How far from St Helena to the Gate of Heaven's Grace?'
That no one knows – that no one knows – and no one ever will.
But fold your hands across your heart and cover up your face,
And after all your trapesings, child, lie still!

I first discovered this poem of Kipling's in one of the best of all anthologies, Field-Marshal Wavell's Other Men's Flowers. *As Wavell himself mentions, one verse is out of chronological order: Trafalgar predated Austerlitz by six weeks. But it doesn't seem to matter very much.*

La vie est vaine,
Un peu d'amour,
Un peu de peine,
Et puis, bonjour!

La vie est brève,
Un peu d'espoir,
Un peu de rêve,
Et puis, bonsoir!

Victor Hugo

[But – and I hate to say it – see now p. 189.]

Bonus

Colin Thubron has kindly sent me a copy of a notice issued in Saudi Arabia during the Gulf War of 1990–91:

BY THE NAME OF ALLAH THE MOST GREACIOUS & MOST MERCIFULL
General Direction and Precautions in Case if there is an Attack of Poisonous Gass

A. VISIBLE SYMPTOMS:
- (1) you find birds dropping from trees.
- (2) Cats, Dogs, People choking, dropping.
- (3) Car crashing, car accidents.
- (4) Everything Abnormal.
- (5) Visible Fog/Mist in the Air.

B. WHAT YOU SHOULD DO:
- (1) if you are out of your House/Office, on the Road, forget that there is any solution, Pray Allah the ALL-mighty for help who can do miracles.
- (2) If you are inside House/Office, do undermentioned:
  - (a) Close all doors, windows, ventilation fans, in toilets, kitchens and al other places which allows extra outside Air in your flat/Office or Circulate any Gas.
  - (b) Close air conditioners immediately.
  - (c) Don't open your door, windows for whatever reason there is, don't allow anybody to enter or go out of the place.
  - (d) Wear cloths with long sleeves, long pants, socks, Gloves, Scarf etc, cover your head and face with wet blanket or towel.
  - (e) Don't try to run away by your car, it will bring you and other people more problems and it may cause accidents.
  - (f) Hope that the Gas effect will disappear within two hours INSHALLAH.

C. IF YOU HAVE UNDERMENTIONED SYMPTOMS, WHAT YOU MAY DO:
- (1) Blisters on skin – don't burst or scrach.
- (2) Headache – Loose of co-ordination, get shower immediately, turn water, wash off continuously for some time.

(3) Relax as much as you can to reduce your demand of Air.

(4) It is much more better to stay inside House and most important that don't get Hot Temper, be cool minded.

TYPES OF GAS:

A: Mustard Gas
  – Toxic irritent-blister on skin, inflimmations, etc.
  – Make your lungs blood, slow death.
  – Water soluble, use wet towel to cover face and head, stay in shower.
  – Lasts one to two hours.

B: Cyanide
  – Highly Hemotoxic (highly poisonuous in blood).
  – No external inflamation etc. works inside.
  – Loss of co-ordination, dizziness, difficulty in breathing, pain.
  – Water soluble, use wet towel to cover face and head, stay in shower.
  – Last upto one hour.

C: Nerve Gas (Various Types)
  – Neurotoxi – work on neurves, system.
  – Quick acting.
  – Loss brain control on neurves, shaking blurrod vising, choking etc.
  – best filtered. via atrivated carbon or charcoal.
  – Wet cloth, mask may help – Disperade quickly last 30 minutes maximum.

The above information is given only for your reference and understanding but meantime we pray Allah the ALL Mighty to save all Islam and
Muslims from this and such kinds of other problems. Best Regards . . .

A
Christmas
Cracker

1992

From the Peterborough Echo, *1977:*

THE CEREMONY AT THE LIBRARY

Crowland's Silver
Jubilee Committee
finally wound up on
Thursday evening with
a presentation ceremony
at the library.

The jubilee fund, des-
cribed by chairman
Frank Parnell as 'one
of the finest efforts in
Lincolnshire', fremony
at the library.

The jubilee fund, des-
cribed by chairman
Frank Parnell as 'one
remony atremony aremony
at the library.'

The jubremony at the
library.

Tremony at remony at the
library.

Thrremony at tremony at
the liremony at the lib-
raremony at the library.

Theremony at the library.

The jubilee fund,
described by chairman
Frank Premony rremony at
the liremony atremony at
tremony at the library.

Tremorremony at the lib-
rary remony at the library.

The jubilee fund.
described by chairman

Frank Parnell as 'one of
the finest efforts in
Lincolnshire', fa he
latched onto a through
ball. Although he was
hauled down by the
keeper he still managed
to stroke the ball home.

For I will consider my cat Jeoffrey,
For he is the servant of the living God, duly and daily serving him.

Christopher Smart

These curiously touching lines are taken from Jubilate Agno, *a long religious poem which Smart described as 'my Magnificat' (he was not, I think, referring to Jeoffrey) and which he wrote during a four-year incarceration in Bedlam. According to the* Oxford Companion to English Literature, *'his derangement took the form of a compulsion to public prayer, which occasioned the famous comment of Dr Johnson: "I'd as lief pray with Kit Smart as anyone else." ' Johnson, as Boswell tells us, was another cat-lover:*

I shall never forget the indulgence with which Dr Johnson treated Hodge, his cat; for whom he himself used to go out and buy oysters lest the servants, having that trouble, should take a dislike to the poor creature. I am unluckily one of those who have an antipathy to a cat, so that I am uneasy when in the room with one, and I own I frequently suffered a good deal from the presence of the same Hodge.

I recollect him one day scrambling up Dr Johnson's breast apparently with much satisfaction while my friend, smiling and half-whistling, rubbed down his back and pulled him by the tail and when I observed he was a fine cat, saying, 'Why yes, Sir, but then I have had cats that I liked better than this,' and then, as if perceiving Hodge to be out of countenance, adding, 'but he is a very fine cat, a very fine cat indeed.'

How odd, when one comes to think about it, that oysters were the food of the very poor right up until the middle of the nineteenth century. 'Bless me,' said Sam Weller, 'if I don't think that when a man's wery poor he doesn't rush out and eat oysters out of sheer desperation'. John Parker – whose name has occurred frequently in these Crackers – reminds me that when Sydney Smith first went to Edinburgh to work on the Review, *his Scottish servants drew up a written undertaking that they should not have to eat salmon more than three times a week.*

*These thoughts of C. P. Cavafy (or others very like them) must, I suspect, occupy the minds of a good many soldiers and statesmen in the western world today –
though they may not express them with quite such elegance:*

What does this sudden uneasiness mean,
   and this confusion? (How grave their faces have become!)
Why are the streets and squares rapidly emptying,
   and why is everyone going back home, so lost in thought?
     Because it is night and the barbarians have not come;
     And some men have arrived from the frontiers
     and they say that barbarians don't exist any longer.
And now what will become of us without barbarians?
     They were a kind of solution.

(Tr. J. Mavrogordato)

In America, every schoolboy can – or could, fifty years ago – recite Abraham Lincoln's Gettysburg address by heart; in England it is hardly known at all. Yet it should be, for it is one of the most perfect short speeches ever made.

Fourscore and seven years ago our fathers brought forth upon this continent a new nation, dedicated to the proposition that all men are created equal. Now we are engaged in a great civil war, testing whether that nation, or any nation so conceived and so dedicated, can long endure. We are met on a great battlefield of that war. We have come to dedicate a portion of that field as a final resting-place of those who here gave their lives that that nation might live. It is altogether fitting and proper that we should do this. But in a larger sense we cannot dedicate, we cannot consecrate, we cannot hallow this ground. The brave men, living and dead, who struggled here, have consecrated it far above our power to add or detract. The world will little note, nor long remember, what we say here, but it can never forget what they did here. It is for us, the living, rather to be dedicated here to the unfinished work they have thus far so nobly advanced. It is rather for us to be here dedicated to the great task remaining before us, that from these honoured dead we take increased devotion to that cause for which they here gave the last full measure of devotion; that we here highly resolve that the dead shall not have died in vain, that this nation, under God, shall have a new birth of freedom; and that government of the people, by the people, for the people, shall not perish from the earth.

Those words were spoken at the ceremony of dedication of the National Cemetery at Gettysburg on 19 November 1863. A Chicago newspaper, reporting it, wrote:

We did not conceive it possible that even he would produce an address so slipshod, so loose-joined, so puerile – not alone in literary construction, but in its ideas, its sentiments, its grasp . . . By the side of it, mediocrity is superb.

Edwin Markham showed himself a good deal more perceptive when he wrote the following words for the dedication of the Lincoln Memorial in Washington DC in 1922:

> The colour of the ground was in him, the red earth,
> The smack and tang of elemental things.
>   Sprung from the West,
> He drank the valorous youth of a new world.
> The strength of virgin forests braced his mind,

The hush of spacious prairies stilled his soul.
His words were oaks in acorns; and his thoughts
Were roots that firmly gripped the granite truth.

At the time of the wedding of the Prince and Princess of Wales in 1981 my mother used gleefully to refer to herself as 'the wrong Lady Diana'. Here is a letter from a far more unfortunate namesake, the wrong Franz Schubert (1768–1824), a composer of church music at the court of Saxony. It was addressed to Messrs Breitkopf and Härtel, the Leipzig music publishers, who had inadvertently returned to him the right Franz Schubert's manuscript of Erlkönig:

Dresden, 18 April 1817

Dear Friend,

. . . I must also inform you that some ten days ago I received your esteemed letter with which you enclosed the manuscript of Goethe's *Erlkönig*, alleged to have been set by me. With the greatest astonishment I beg to assure you that I never composed this cantata. I shall retain it in my possession in order to find out if possible who was so ill-mannered as to send you such trash; and who is the fellow who has taken my name in vain . . .

Your most obliged friend and brother

Franz Schubert
His Majesty's Composer of Sacred Music

It's a long time – seven years, to be precise – since we've had any Shakespeare in the Crackers; understandably, perhaps, because once one starts on him it's very hard to stop.

> Now does he feel
> The secret murders sticking on his hands

Macbeth

> O Proserpina,
> For the flowers now, that (frighted) thou let'st fall
> From Dis's waggon! daffodils
> That come before the swallow dares, and take
> The winds of March with beauty; violets (dim,
> But sweeter than the lids of Juno's eyes . . .)

The Winter's Tale

And talking of Proserpina, what about those three marvellous lines from the Purgatorio?

> Tu mi fai rimembrar dove e qual era
> Proserpina, nel tempo che perdetta
> La madre lei, ed ella primavera.

A letter to The Times, *published on 6 March 1985:*

Sir,

Miss Catherine J. Clark (March 2) need agonize no longer over the etiquette governing revolving doors. Whenever faced by this problem and a lady is about to approach the doors, I boldly enter first and push the doors for her; but in order to give the lady precedence of ingress I describe a full circle before effecting my final entry. This seems to puzzle hotel porters, but it is a clear statement, Sir, that chivalry is not dead.

Yours faithfully

Carlo Ardito

A poem by Arthur Guiterman, written in response to a news report that Mrs John Masefield, having arrived in England with her husband from America, had announced that the crossing was 'too uppy-downy' and that Mr Masefield was ill:

I must go down to the seas again, where the billows romp and reel,
So all I ask is a large ship that rides on an even keel;
And a mild breeze, and a broad deck, with a slight list to leeward,
And a clean chair in a snug nook and a nice, kind steward.

I must go down to the seas again, the sport of wind and tide,
As the grey wave and the green wave play leapfrog over the side;
And all I want is a glassy calm with a bone-dry scupper,
And a good book, and a warm rug, and a light, plain supper.

I must go down to the seas again, though there I'm a total loss,
And can't say which is worst – the pitch, the plunge, the roll, the toss.
But all I ask is a safe retreat in a bar well tended,
And a soft berth and a smooth course till the long trip's ended.

Tu m'as rendu fades tous les hommes, et médiocres tous les destins.

These words of Henry de Montherlant (though from which novel or play I have been unable to discover) must be the most perfect compliment that any woman could pay to her husband. They were, I understand, frequently on the lips of Mrs Robert Maxwell. One sees, in a way, what she meant.

John Sparrow, former Warden of All Souls, died on 24 January 1992. In the 1980 Cracker I included his poem on S. Maria della Salute in Venice, raising as it did the intriguing question – still unsolved – of the identity of the iron-founders Theodore and Hasselquist. Here, in his memory, are two more little jeux d'esprit:

ENTSAGEN SOLLST DU

He raised the glittering goblet to his lips
And drank the ambrosial liquid to the dregs;
He kissed the face that launched a thousand ships –
And killed the goose that laid the golden eggs.

TO AN ANGEL IN THE HOUSE

A pat on the head
Sends me happy to bed,
I wish – how I wish – you'd do *that* more!
Cold words and neglect
Leave me wretched and wrecked:
Don't send me to Coventry – pat more!

John also wrote his own epitaph:

Here, with his talents in a napkin hid,
Lies one who much designed and nothing did.
Deferring and postponing day by day
He quite procrastinated life away,
And when at last the summons came to die
With his last breath put off mortality.

Sir Henry Norreys – whose father had been executed by Henry VIII as an alleged lover of Anne Boleyn – married, some time before 1545, Marjorie Williams of Rycote in Oxfordshire, through whom he later inherited the manor and estate. The couple were much beloved of Queen Elizabeth I, who often stayed at Rycote and who nicknamed the raven-haired Lady Norreys her 'black crow'. When in September 1592 the Queen paid her last visit to her old friends, Sir Henry received her with the traditional speech of welcome – he was now nearing seventy – in which he declared:

I meane not to recount my service, but to tell Your Majesty that I am past al service, save devotion. My horse, mine armour, my shielde, my sworde, the riches of a young souldier, and an old souldier's reliques, I should here offer to your Highnesse; but my four boies have stalled them from me, vowing themselves to armes, and leaving me to my prayers. This is their resolution, and my desire, that their lives may be imployed wholy in your service, and their deathes be their vowes sacrifice. Their deathes, the rumour of which hath so often affrighted the Crowe my wife, that her hart hath bene as black as her feathers. I know not whether it be affection or fondness, but the Crowe thinketh her owne birds the fairest, because to her they are the dearest.

I came upon this text in the admirable guide-book to Rycote Chapel. Its author, Mr John Salmon, continues:

On the following Sunday morning Elizabeth went into the garden where 'sweete musicke' was played, and there she received four letters, one from Ireland, another from Flanders and two from Brittany, each accompanied by some valuable little gift. They were from the four Norreys sons serving abroad. The Norreyses had six sons in all. The eldest, William, had already died on active service in Ireland in 1579. Four others were to die in similar circumstances, three in Ireland and one in Brittany, before their father's death ... When the second son, John, died in Ireland in 1597 Elizabeth sent a formal letter to Lady Norreys to which she added a postscript in her own hand. 'Myne owne Crowe, harme not thyselfe for booteles healpe; but shewe a good example, to comfort your dolorous yokefellow.'

The old couple, though buried at Rycote, are commemorated by a splendid monument in St Andrew's Chapel in Westminster Abbey, their six lovely sons kneeling around them.

A lady from the Bosphorus with eyes as black as phosphorus
Once wed the wealthy bailiff of the Caliph of Kelat;
Though diligent and zealous, he soon fell a prey to jealousy –
Considering her beauty, 'twas his duty to do that.

It must be mentioned casually that blue as lapis lazuli
He dyed his hair, his lashes, his moustaches and his beard;
And just because he did it, he aroused his wife's timidity –
Her terror she dissembled, but she trembled when he neared.

A state so insalubrious soon made her quite lugubrious,
On top of which she missed her little sister, Mary Anne;
So asked, could she invite her to come down and spend a night or
    two?
Her husband answered rightly – and politely – 'Sure you can.'

When business would necessitate a journey, he would hesitate,
But, fearing to disgust her, would entrust her with his keys,
Remarking to her prayerfully, 'Now mind you use them carefully;
Don't look what I deposit in the closet, if you please!'

Bluebeard, the Monday following, his jealous feelings swallowing,
Packed all his things together in a leather-lined valise,
And, lying reprehensibly, he started off – ostensibly
To travel, and to learn a bit of Smyrna and of Greece.

His wife made but a cursory inspection of the nursery;
The kitchen and the airy little dairy were a bore;
Likewise the small and scanty rooms, the billiard halls and
    ante-rooms;
But not the interdicted and restricted little door.

Since all her curiosity was centred on the closet he'd
So distantly, insistently, forbidden her to see,
The maiden disobedient did something inexpedient –
And in the keyhole tiny turned the shiny little key.

Then, standing back impulsively, she cried aloud convulsively –
Ten heads, of wives he'd wedded and beheaded, met her eye;
And turning round quite terrified, her darkest fears were verified:
For Bluebeard stood behind her – come to find her on the sly.

Then, fearing she was fated to be soon decapitated too,
She telegraphed her brothers (and some others) what she feared;
And sister Anne looked out for them in readiness to shout for them
Whenever in the distance with assistance they appeared.

But only through the battlement she saw some dust, which cattle
  meant . . .
This ordinary story isn't gory, just a jest;
But here's the truth unqualified: Bluebeard would not be mollified –
Her head is in the bloody little study, with the rest.

*My friend Michael Rogers, who first introduced me to this little masterpiece, tells
me that he believes it to be by Stephen Leacock, but cannot be sure. Can any
reader confirm, I wonder?*

Two ghost stories from John Aubrey's Miscellanies. *The first – which is almost too well known – must be the shortest in the language:*

Anno 1670, not far from *Cyrencester*, was an Apparition: Being demanded, whether a good Spirit or a bad? returned no answer, but disappeared with a curious Perfume and a most melodious Twang. Mr W. *Lilly* believes it was a Farie.

The second – not very much longer – concerns Major-General the first Lord Middleton:

This Lord Middleton had a great Friendship with the Laird Bocconi, and they had made an Agreement, That the first of them that Died, should appear to the other in extremity. The Lord Middleton was taken Prisoner at Worcester Fight, and was Prisoner in the Tower of London under Three Locks. Lying in his Bed pensive, Bocconi appeared to him; my Lord Middleton asked him if he were dead or alive: he said, Dead, and that he was a Ghost; and told him, that within Three Days he should escape, and he did so, in his Wives Cloaths. When he had done his Message, he gave a Frisk, and said,

> Givenni givanni 'tis very strange,
> In the World to see so sudden a Change.

And then gathered up and vanished.

Harriet's virginity they marvelled over a great deal. It seemed a privilege to have it under the same roof. They were always kindly enquiring after it as if it were a sick relative. It must not be bestowed lightly, they advised. It must not be bestowed at all, Mrs Brimpton said.

Elizabeth Taylor,
A Game of Hide and Seek

Mark but this flea, and mark in this,
How little that which thou deny'st me is;
It suck'd me first, and now sucks thee,
And in this flea, our two bloods mingled be;
Thou know'st that this cannot be said
A sin, nor shame, nor loss of maidenhead,
    Yet this enjoys before it woo,
      And pamper'd swells with one blood made of two,
      And this, alas, is more than we would do.

Oh stay, three lives in one flea spare,
Where we almost, yea more than married are.
This flea is you and I, and this
Our marriage bed, and marriage temple is;
Though parents grudge, and you, we're met
And cloistered in these living walls of jet.
    Though use make you apt to kill me,
      Let not to that, self-murder added be,
      And sacrilege, three sins in killing three.

Cruel and sudden, hast thou since
Purpled thy nail, in blood of innocence?
Wherein could this flea guilty be,
Except in that drop which it suck'd from thee?
Yet thou triumph'st, and say'st that thou
Find'st not thyself, not me the weaker now;
    'Tis true, then learn, how false fears be;
      Just so much honour, when thou yield'st to me,
      Will waste, as this flea's death took life from thee.

John Donne

Here is one of my favourite entries in Who's Who, *transcribed from the 1987 edition. (The subject/author died the following year.) I particularly love the way he paces himself: starting slowly and – let's face it – fairly boringly, then building up the surprises in a steady crescendo:*

RANKIN, Sir Hugh (Charles Rhys), 3rd Bt., *cr.* 1898; FSA Scot. 1948; Member, Standing Council of the Baronetage, since 1979; Representative to District Council Perth CC (Eastern District) 1949, Perth CC 1950; Council for Boro' of Rathray and Blairgowrie, 1949; joined RASC as 2nd Lieut, May 1940, at age of 41 years; Captain 1940–45, India; sheep farming and is a judge of sheep at prominent shows; formerly Senior Vice-President of the Western Islamic Association; a former Vice-President of Scottish National Liberal Association; has lived during the reigns of six sovereigns; *b.* 8 Aug 1899; *er. s.* of Sir Reginald Rankin, 2nd Bt., and Hon. Nest Rice (*d.* 1943), 2nd *d.* of Baron Dynevor; changed his names by Scotch law in July 1946 to above; *s.* father 1931; *m.* 1932, Helen Margaret (*d.* 1945), *e.d.* of Sir Charles Stewart, KBE, 1st Public Trustee, and *widow* of Capt. Colin Campbell, Scots Guards; *m.* 1946, Robina Kelly, FSA (Scot.), SRN, Cordon Bleu (Edin.), Crieff, Perthshire. *Educ:* Harrow. Served in 1st Royal Dragoon Guards in Sinn Feinn [*sic*] Campaign, 1920–22 (oldest surviving mem.); Ex-Pres. Clun Forest Sheep Breeders Assoc., 1928, and their representative to National Sheep Breeders Association that year; whole-time 'piece-work' shearer in W. Australia, covering area between Bunbury and Broome, 1929–31; in 1938 was a representative on committee of British sheep breeders in London appointed to petition Government *re* sheep industry. Runner-up All Britain Sheep Judging Competition (6,000 entrants), 1962. A writer on agricultural stock; expert on Highland problems; was Brit. Rep., 1937, to 1st all European Muslim Congress at Geneva; a practising Non-Theistic Theravada Buddhist since 1944, and performed Holy Buddhist Pilgrimage, Nov. 1944, the 2nd Britisher to do so; Vice-Pres. World's Buddhist Assoc., 1945. Joined Labour Party 1939 and holds extreme political views; has been a Dominion Home Ruler for Scotland, member of Scottish National Party; joined Scottish Communist Party, 1945, resigned 1980; Welsh Republican Nationalist and Welsh speaker; now left-side Labour; also zealous SNP who desires an independent Red Republic of all Scotland, exc. Orkneys and Shetlands. Has made archaeological discoveries in Dumfries, 1977– . Mem. Roy. Inst. and Roy. Soc. of Arts; is Hereditary Piper of the Clan Maclaine. News of the World Kt of the Road (for courtesy in motor driving). Broadsword Champion of British Army (Cavalry), 1921. *Publications:* articles in agricultural publications, etc. *Recreations:* golf (holds an amateur record amongst golfers of Gt.

Britain in having played on 382 separate courses of UK and Eire), shooting, coarse fishing, hunting, motoring, cycling on mountain tracks to tops of British mountains (Pres. Rough Stuff Cycling Assoc., 1956); study of ancient track ways; bowls, tennis, archaeology (wife and himself are only persons who have crawled under dwarf fir forest for last ½ mile of most northerly known section of any Roman road in Europe, terminating opposite end of Kirriemuir Golf Course), study of domestic animals, speaking on politics, especially *re* Scottish Home Rule and Highland problems . . .

Remember now thy Creator in the days of thy youth, while the evil days come not, nor the years draw nigh, when thou shalt say, I have no pleasure in them;

While the sun, or the light, or the moon, or the stars, be not darkened, nor the clouds return after the rain;

In the day when the keepers of the house shall tremble, and the strong men shall bow themselves, and the grinders cease because they are few, and those that look out of the windows be darkened.

And the doors shall be shut in the streets, when the sound of the grinding is low, and he shall rise up at the voice of the bird, and all the daughters of musick shall be brought low;

Also when they shall be afraid of that which is high, and fears shall be in the way, and the almond tree shall flourish, and the grasshopper shall be a burden, and desire shall fail: because man goeth to his long home, and the mourners go about the streets:

Or ever the silver cord be loosed, or the golden bowl be broken, or the pitcher be broken at the fountain, or the wheel broken at the cistern.

Then shall the dust return to the earth as it was: and the spirit shall return unto God who gave it.

Ecclesiastes, xii, 1–7

In an article that she was reading in the New Yorker *my friend Mary Lutyens saw a quotation from Samuel Butler's* The Way of All Flesh:

'Tis better to have loved and lost than never to have lost at all.

Printing it, the New Yorker *had thought it had spotted a howler, and that the passage was a misquotation from Tennyson's* In Memoriam:

'Tis better to have loved and lost/Than never to have loved at all.

and had made some snide comment. To Mary's letter pointing out that it was the magazine that had made a fool of itself, she received the following reply:

October 29, 1987

Dear Mrs Lutyens,

Thank you for your note, and for reading our pages so attentively. It is always a pleasure to hear from a well-informed reader, although in this case the pleasure is bittersweet.

You are, of course, quite right about the quotation from Samuel Butler. We do pride ourselves on our accuracy, but you know what pride goeth before. The measures we take to avoid mistakes are unusually thorough, but not, as you see, foolproof.

It is particularly mortifying to have made an accusation of error which is itself erroneous. It is the kind of mistake which can only be made in presumptuousness. We are chagrined, we are contrite, and we are genuinely grateful to you for correcting us.

We cannot help thinking that the shade of Samuel Butler must be enjoying our discomfiture. We feel a little like Theobald Pontifex confounded.

Sincerely yours,

Owen Ketherry.

P.S. We cannot answer your question about the number of readers who spotted the error, because their letters are still pouring in every day.

Last year's Cracker contained the epitaph of George Routleigh, watchmaker, from Lydford in Devon. Compare the following, from High Wycombe:

Of no distemper,
Of no blast he died,
But fell,
Like Autumn's fruit
That mellows long,
Even wondered at
Because he dropt not sooner.
Providence seemed to wind him up
For fourscore years,
Yet ran he nine winters more;
Till, like a clock
Worn out with repeating time,
The wheels of weary life
At last stood still.

In Memory of John ABDIDGE, Alderman.
Died 1785.

The greatest pleasure I know is to do a good action by stealth and have it found out by accident.

Charles Lamb

To David and Hazel Langford I am indebted for 'Hazel's Language Lessons, culled from her awesome collection of weird dictionaries'. Here are a few of the choicer items:

HAUSA: *'Yan garkuwa*. Professional beggars living by threatening to do obscene acts unless given alms.

HINDUSTANI: *Dhaunchá*. The sum of four times a number or quantity added to its half: the *pahárá*, or multiplication table of 4½ times.

JAPANESE: *Uguisu no tani-watari*. 1. A nightingale jumping back and forth over a narrow valley; 2. One man in bed with two women.
Sakasa-kurage. 1. An upside-down jellyfish; 2. A one-night-stand hotel.

KIKUYU: *Komaria*. To touch somebody reprovingly or threateningly with a stick and say 'wee!'
Ruuka. To become uncircumcised.

KURDISH: *Binêsk*. What remains of a tablet of soap when it is nearly used up.

MARATHI: *Baccedha*. The bother, fuss and vexation attendant upon the bringing up of children.
Avlyachi mot. A very loose and patched-up union based on no consolidation of interests and with an ever-present tendency to separation.

SESUTO: *Malito*. Something which a person lets fall and which his cousin can pick up and keep if the owner does not say ngaele. [*Ngaele* not listed in dictionary]

SINHALESE: *Akshauhiaí*. An army consisting of 21,870 elephants, 21,870 chariots, 65,610 horses and 109,350 foot-soldiers.

SWAHILI: *Hatinafsi*. Used of a person taking an action without consulting anybody because he thinks they may try to persuade him not to do it.

[*NB Referring to the Kikuyu entry above, John Parker (there he goes again) points out that 'to become uncircumcised' is also good New Testament Greek – though I still I don't understand how you do it. See, anyway, I Corinthians 1, vii, 18.*]

Authorities:
Dictionary of the Hausa Language by R. C. Abraham, London, 2nd edn, 1962
The Student's Romanised Practical Dictionary, Allahabad, 1941

Japanese in Action by Jack Seward, Tokyo, 1968

Kikuyu–English Dictionary, ed. T. G. Benson, Oxford, 1964

A Kurdish-English Dictionary, by T. Wahby and C. J. Edmonds, Oxford, 1966

The Arya-Bhushan School Dictionary, by Shridhar Ganesh Vaze, BA, 1928

Sesuto-English Vocabulary, Société des Missions Evangéliques de Paris, Cape Town, 1904

Sinhalese–English Dictionary, ed. for the University of Ceylon by M. D. Ratnasuriya and P. B. F. Wijeratne, Colombo, 1949

A Standard Swahili–English Dictionary, Oxford, 1939

Denkt ihr an mich ein Augenblickchen nur;
Ich werde Zeit genug an Euch zu denken haben.

Think you of me for just a moment only;
I shall have time enough to think of you.

Goethe,
Faust

Compare that lovely couplet from Sephestia's Song to her Child, *by Robert Greene:*

Weep not, my wanton, smile upon my knee,
When thou art old, there's grief enough for thee.

In the first chapter of her book Venice Observed, *Mary McCarthy points out that 'nothing can be said here (including this statement) that has not been said before'. Shortly afterwards, however, she herself produces what I suspect to be an entirely original idea – which, incidentally, provides an intriguing answer to a problem that has long had me baffled.*

Why should it be beautiful at all? Why should Venice, aside from its situation, be a place of enchantment? One appears to be confronted with a paradox. A commercial people who lived solely for gain – how could they create a city of fantasy, lovely as a dream or fairy-tale? This is the central puzzle of Venice, the stumbling-block that one keeps coming up against if one tries to *think* about her history together with the visual fact that is there before one's eyes. It cannot be that Venice is a happy accident or a trick of light. I have thought about this a long time, but now it occurs to me that, as with most puzzles, the clue to the answer lies in the way the question is framed. 'Lovely as a dream or fairy-tale . . .' There is no contradiction, once you stop to think what images of beauty arise from fairy-tales. They are images of money. Gold, caskets of gold, caskets of silver, the miller's daughter spinning gold all night long, thanks to Rumpelstiltskin, the cave of Ali Baba stored with stolen gold and silver, the underground garden in which Aladdin found jewels growing on trees, so that he could gather them in his hands, rubies and diamonds and emeralds, the Queen's lovely daughter whose hair is black as ebony and lips are red as rubies, treasure buried in the forest, treasure guarded by dogs with eyes as big as carbuncles, treasure guarded by a Beast – this is the spirit of the enchantment under which Venice lies, pearly and roseate, like the Sleeping Beauty, changeless throughout the centuries, arrested, while the concrete forest of the modern world grows up around her.

A wholly materialist city is nothing but a dream incarnate. Venice is the world's unconscious: a miser's glittering hoard, guarded by a Beast whose eyes are made of white agate, and by a saint who is really a prince who has just slain a dragon.

LULLABY

Drowsily, dreamily, dreamily, drowsily,
Calmly and quietly counting the cowsily,
Sleepily, languidly, languidly, sleepily,
Peeping at stiles and assessing the sheepily,
Snoozily, snorily, snorily, snoozily,
Why keep awake when they've run out of boozily?

Roger Till

Bonus

From the obituary of the third Lord Moynihan: Daily Telegraph, 26 November 1991:

The third Lord Moynihan, who has died in Manila, aged fifty-five, provided, through his character and career, ample ammunition for critics of the hereditary principle. His chief occupations were bongo-drummer, confidence trickster, brothel-keeper, drug-smuggler and police informer, but 'Tony' Moynihan also claimed other areas of expertise – as 'professional negotiator', 'international diplomatic courier', 'currency manipulator' and 'authority on rock and roll' . . .

The first time he ran away was in 1956, to Australia. There were two reasons for his flight. The first was to elude his father's fury over a liaison with a Soho nightclub waitress. The second was to escape his wife, an actress and sometime nude model; they had married secretly the previous year, and she had now taken out a summons against him for assault. Her father had made a similar complaint – 'I regret to say I gave him a swift right upper-cut', Moynihan announced from Australia. The idea was that he should work on his uncle's sheep farm in the bush, but after five days he ran away to Sydney, where he made his debut as a banjo-player and met the Malayan fire-eater's assistant who was to become his second wife . . .

After he succeeded his father in the peerage in 1965, Moynihan took the Liberal whip in the House of Lords, where he was principally concerned in arguing that Gibraltar be given to Spain. The House was not impressed. In 1968 Lord Boothby interrupted one of Moynihan's speeches: 'My Lords, the noble Lord has bored us stiff for nearly three-quarters of an hour. I beg to move that he no longer be heard.'

Moynihan's business career and personal finances had meanwhile given rise to a number of misunderstandings. By 1970 he faced fifty-seven charges – among them fraudulent trading, false pretences, fraud against a gaming casino and the purchase of a Rolls-Royce motor-car with a worthless cheque. To avoid disaster he fled once more, this time to Spain . . .

In 1968 he had married for a third time – another belly-dancer, this time a Filipino – and the new Lady Moynihan's family had a chain of massage parlours in Manila, where Moynihan remained for much of the rest of his life . . . As the 1970s wore on he found employment in the narcotics trade, as well as in fraud and prostitution . . . He continued his life as a Filipino pimp under the patronage of President Marcos – 'my drinking chum', as he called him. Marcos apparently shielded him from prosecution over the murder of a nightclub owner (who had married one of Moynihan's ex-wives). At one stage he ran a brothel within 100 yards of the British Ambassador's residence . . .

Anthony Patrick Andrew Cairne Berkeley Moynihan was born on February 2 1936, the elder son of Patrick Moynihan, a barrister and stockbroker who succeeded to the barony of Moynihan later that year . . . Young Tony was educated at Stowe and did his National Service in the Coldstream Guards; it was his last contact with respectability, and he was inclined to reminisce over it in his cups . . .

In Manila, to which he returned after his sojourn in America, Moynihan lived in the suburbs in a heavily fortified house with a swimming pool, and had as his base in the city a brothel named the Yellow Brick Road. 'I just sit back and collect the money,' he said. 'The girls do all the work.'

He frequently spoke of returning to England – 'to clear my name,' as he put it. 'I miss things like decent roast beef and good newspapers, the civilized way of life' . . .

Moynihan is reported to have been married five times, and to have fathered various children. The heir to the barony appears to be his son Daniel, born in February this year.

A
Christmas
Cracker

1993

My old friend Sir James Richards died last year. Here, in his memory, is a section from the opening paragraphs of his autobiography, Memoirs of an Unjust Fella:

Whenever I was brought by my parents from our home in London to visit the Rectory at Dungannon, no sooner had we arrived at the end of a tiring journey by rail and sea than I was summoned into my grandfather's study: 'Now my boy, let me hear you recite the Glorious Pious.' Terrifying would be his wrath if I ever faltered.

It was the first thing I ever learned by heart, and I can remember it to this day:

Here's to the glorious pious and immortal memory of King William Prince of Orange who saved us from Rome Romery Popes Popery brass money and wooden shoes. Whoever will not drink this toast may he be rammed damned and double jammed down the great gun of Athlone and thence shot into the air to make sparables for the shoes of Orangemen on the twelfth of July in the morning.

I never dared to inquire what sparables were.

The Oxford English Dictionary *would have told him:*

A small headless wedge-shaped iron nail (stouter than a *sprig*), used in the soles and heels of boots and shoes.

[My friend (and sonneteer extraordinary) Jim Hacobian adds that the sparable is so called from its resemblance in shape to a sparrow's bill.]

Publication in the Cracker *of the Glorious Pious elicited – but alas, I no longer know from whom – an interesting variant:*

To the Glorious, Pious and Immortal memory of Willy the Three; who saved us from Rogues and Roguery, Knaves and Knavery, Popes and Popery; from Brass Monkeys and Wooden Shoes. And whoever denies this toast, may he be slammed, jammed and crammed into the muzzle of the Great Gun of Athlone, and the gun fired into the Pope's belly, and the Pope into the Devil's belly, and the Devil into Hell, and the door locked and the key in an Orangeman's pocket for ever. And may we never lack a brisk Protestant boy to kick the arse of a papist; and here's a fart for the Bishop of Cork.

Just a decade ago, in the 1983 Cracker, *I included Henry Reed's marvellous poem from* Lessons of the War, *'Today we have Naming of Parts'. Here is another poem of his, perhaps not quite so well known. It is called 'Judging Distances':*

Not only how far away, but the way that you say it
Is very important. Perhaps you may never get
The knack of judging a distance, but at least you know
How to report on a landscape: the central sector,
The right of arc and that, which we had last Tuesday,
    And at least you know

That maps are of time, not place, so far as the Army
Happens to be concerned – the reason being,
Is one which need not delay us. Again you know
There are three kinds of tree, three only, the fir and the poplar,
And those which have bushy tops to; and lastly
    That things only seem to be things.

A barn is not called a barn, to put it more plainly,
Or a field in the distance, where sheep may be safely grazing.
You must never be over-sure. You must say, when reporting,
At five o'clock in the central sector is a dozen
Of what appear to be animals; whatever you do,
    Don't call the bleeders *sheep.*

I am sure that's quite clear; and suppose, for the sake of example,
The one at the end, asleep, endeavours to tell us
What he sees over there to the west, and how far away,
After first having come to attention. There to the west,
On the fields of summer the sun and the shadows bestow
    Vestments of purple and gold.

The still white dwellings are like a mirage in the heat,
And under the swaying elms a man and a woman
Lie gently together. Which is, perhaps, only to say
That there is a row of houses to the left of arc,
And that under some poplars a pair of what appear to be humans
    Appear to be loving.

Well that, for an answer, is what we might rightly call
Moderately satisfactory only, the reason being,
Is that two things have been omitted, and those are important.
The human beings, now: in what direction are they,
And how far away, would you say? And do not forget
    There may be dead ground in between.

There may be dead ground in between; and I may not have got
The knack of judging a distance; I will only venture
A guess that perhaps between me and the apparent lovers,
(Who, incidentally, appear by now to have finished)
At seven o'clock from the houses, is roughly a distance
   Of about one year and a half.

The Diaries of Wilfrid Blunt contain an enjoyable anecdote about my putative grandfather – and, some say, Lady Thatcher's – Harry Cust:

Harry was at Lynn with Asquith and Herbert Gladstone, and the suffragettes were striking Asquith in the face with their fists. Harry intervened as Secretary of the Golf Club (of which he was not a member), telling the women that whatever their dispute with the Prime Minister might be, it was impossible that they should be allowed to walk on the grass, as it was against the regulations of the Club. This impressed them and they desisted from their assaults.

[*Recently I read for the first time* A Backward Glance *by Edith Wharton, which contains this passage:*

One night at dinner in this *milieu* – I think at Lady Ripon's – I found myself next to a man of about thirty-five or forty, whose name I had not caught. We fell into conversation, and within five minutes I was being whirled away on such a quick current of talk as I had not dipped into for many a day. My neighbour moved with dazzling agility from topic to topic, tossing them to and fro like glittering glass balls, always making me share in the game, yet directing it with a practised hand. We soon discovered a common love of letters, and I think it was our main theme that evening. At all events, what I chiefly remember is our having matched, so to speak, the most famous kisses in literature, and my producing as my crowning effect, and to my neighbour's great admiration, the kiss on the stairs in *The Spoils of Poynton* (which I have always thought one of the most moving love-scenes in fiction), while he quoted in exchange the last desperate embrace of Troilus:

> *Injurious Time now with a lover's haste*
> *Crams his rich thievery up, he knows not how;*
> *As many farewells as be stars in heaven . . .*
> *He fumbles up into a loose adieu,*
> *And scants us with a single famished kiss*
> *Distasted with the salt of broken tears.*

Only at the end of the evening did I learn that I had sat next to Harry Cust, one of our most eager and radio-active intelligences in London, unhappily too favoured by fortune to have been forced to canalize his gifts, but a captivating talker and delightful companion in the small circle of his intimates. We struck up a prompt friendship, and thereafter I seldom missed seeing him when I was in London, and keep the memory of delightful lunches and dinners at his picturesque house, looking out over a quiet rose-garden, a stone's throw from the roar of Knightsbridge.]

Two of Pascal's 'Pensées':

Jésus sera en agonie jusqu'à la fin du monde; il ne faut pas dormir pendant ce temps-là.

Le dernier acte est sanglant, quelque belle que soit la comédie en tout le reste: on jette enfin de la terre sur la tête, et en voilà, pour jamais.

Jesus will be in agony until the end of the world; meanwhile, we must not sleep.

The last act is a bloody one, however fine the rest of the comedy: someone throws earth on your head and that is it, for ever.

From The Habits of Good Society, *1851:*

The Bath . . . Besides Champagne, the exquisites of Paris use milk, which is supposed to lend whiteness to the skin. The expense of this luxury is considerably diminished by an arrangement with the milkman, who repurchases the liquid after use.

The Face . . . If a man wear the hair on his face that Nature has given him, in the manner that Nature distributes it, keeps it clean and prevents its overgrowth, he cannot go wrong.

The Handkerchief . . . Can a man of any feeling call on a disconsolate widow for instance, and listen to her woes, without *at least* pulling out his expensive appendage?

Good Manners . . . Of course to knock a man down is never good manners, but there *is* a way of doing it gracefully. Never assail the offender with words, or, when you strike him, use such expressions as 'Take that', etc.

An Elizabethan conceit, said to be by Sir Walter Raleigh, and typical of the sixteenth-century love of ingenious word-play. It can be read either vertically or horizontally – and probably in several other ways as well:

Her face	Her tongue	Her wit
So faire	So sweete	So sharpe
First bent	Then drew	Then hit
Mine eye	Mine eare	My heart
Mine eye	Mine eare	My heart
To like	To learne	To love
Her face	Her tongue	Her wit
Doth lead	Doth teach	Doth move
Oh face	Oh tongue	Oh wit
With frownes	With cheeke	With smarte
Wrong not	Vex not	Wound not
Mine eye	Mine eare	My heart
Mine eye	Mine eare	My heart
To learne	To knowe	To feare
Her face	Her tongue	Her wit
Doth lead	Doth teach	Doth sweare

Sometimes, however – if we are to believe our old friend John Aubrey – Sir Walter was a bit more down to earth:

He loved a wench well; and one time getting up one of the Mayds of Honour up against a tree in a Wood ('twas his first Lady) who seemed at first boarding to be something fearful of her Honour, and modest, she cryed, sweet Sir Walter, what doe you me ask? Will you undoe me? Nay, sweet Sir Walter! Sweet Sir Walter! Sir Walter! At last, as the danger and the pleasure at the same time grew higher, she cryed in the extasey, Swisser Swatter Swisser Swatter. She proved with child, and I doubt not but this Hero tooke care of them both, as also that the Product was more than an ordinary mortal.

Don't be disheartened, young man, we shall hear of you again. You must have loved Nature very much before you could have painted this. Always remember, Sir, that light and shadow never stand still.

> Benjamin West, President of the Royal
> Academy, to the 25-year-old John Constable
> after the RA Exhibitions Committee
> had rejected an early landscape

Two versions of the Lord's Prayer. The Home Counties version was a great favourite at my preparatory school. I hadn't thought of it for half a century, and was delighted to come across it again the other day:

Our Farnham which art in Hendon, Harrow be thy Lane, thy Kingston come, thy Wimbledon in Erith as it is in Heston; give us this Bray our Maidenhead, and forgive us our by-passes as we forgive them that by-pass against us. And lead us not into Thames Ditton, but deliver us from Ewell. For thine is the Kingston, the Purley and the Crawley, for Iver and Iver, Crouch End.

The Politically Correct version comes from the Rev. Kenneth Scott of Thornhill, Ontario:

Our universal chairperson in outer space, your identity enjoys the highest rating on a prioritized selectivity scale. May your sphere of influence take on reality parameters; may your mindset be implemented on this planet as in outer space. Allot to us, at this point in time and on a per diem basis, a sufficient and balanced dietary food intake, and rationalize a disclaimer against our negative feedback; as we rationalize a disclaimer against the negative feedback of others. And deprogram our negative potentialities, but desensitize the impact of the counter-productive force. For yours is the dominant sphere of influence, the ultimate capability, and the highest qualitative analysis rating, at this point in time and extending beyond a limited time-frame. End of message.

The Rev. Gilbert White on rooks:

Just before dusk they return in long strings from the foraging of the day, and rendez-vous by thousands over Selborne-down, where they wheel round in the air, and sport and dive in a playful manner, all the while exerting their voices, and making a loud cawing, which, being blended and softened by the distance that we at the village are below them, becomes a confused noise or chiding; or rather a pleasing murmur, very engaging to the imagination, and not unlike the cry of a pack of hounds in hollow, echoing woods, or the rushing of the wind in tall trees, or the tumbling of the tide upon a pebbly shore. When this ceremony is over, with the last gleam of day, they retire for the night to the deep beechen woods of Tisted and Ropley.

The Natural History of Selborne, 1788

The wind blew out from Bergen from the dawning to the day;
There was wreck of trees and a fall of towers a score of miles away.
And drifted like a livid leaf I go before its tide,
Spewed out of house and stable, beggared of flag and bride.
The heavens are bowed about my head, shouting like seraph wars,
With rains that might put out the sun and clean the sky of stars;
Rains like the fall of ruined seas from secret worlds above,
The roaring of the rains of God none but the lonely love.
Feast in my hall, O foemen, and eat and drink and drain;
You never loved the sun in heaven as I have loved the rain.

The chance of battle changes – so may all battle be;
I stole my lady bride from them, they stole her back from me;
I rent her from her red-roofed hall, I rode, and saw arise
More lovely than the living flowers the hatred in her eyes.
She never loved me, never bent, never was less divine,
The sunset never loved me, the wind was never mine.
Was it all nothing that she stood imperial in duress,
Silence itself made softer with the sweeping of her dress?
O you who drain the cup of life, O you who wear the crown,
You never loved a woman's smile as I have loved her frown.

The wind blew out from Bergen from the dawning to the day;
They ride and run with fifty spears to break and bar my way.
I shall not die alone, alone, but kin to all the powers,
As merry as the ancient sun and fighting like the flowers.
How white their steel, how bright their eyes! I love each laughing
    knave;
Cry high and bid him welcome to the banquet of the brave.
Yes, I will bless them as they bend and love them where they lie,
Where on their skulls the sword I swing falls shattering from the sky;
The hour when death is like a light and blood is like a rose –
You never loved your friends, my friend, as I shall love my foes.

Know you what earth shall lose tonight, what rich, uncounted loans,
What heavy gold of tales untold you bury with my bones?
My loves in deep dim meadows, my ships that rode at ease,

Ruffling the purple plumage of strange and secret seas.
To see this fair earth as it is to me alone was given,
The blow that breaks my skull tonight shall break the dome of
  heaven.
The skies I saw, the trees I saw, after no eye shall see;
Tonight I die the death of God: the stars shall die with me.
One sound shall sunder all the spears and break the trumpet's breath:
You never laughed in all your life as I shall laugh in death.

G. K. Chesterton

The death, aged 100, of my old friend Freya Stark impels me to include something in her memory. The following description of her grandmother comes from the first volume of her autobiography, Traveller's Prelude. *It could have been written by no one else.*

My grandmother as I knew her came into being – always a little of a problem, living with this aunt or that, or in lodgings at the end of long tram or bus routes, in sitting-rooms of dark plush where all the pictures had heavy frames. Here, with small very wrinkled hands, and silk lace carefully and gently draped about her, she radiated her unchanging serenity and charm. She carried about with her that best of grand-motherly atmospheres – a taste of amplitude in Time. No hurry ever came near her. A whole series of episodes in my childhood show her peacefully reading, or dressing, or brushing the long white hair that still could touch her knees, while a babel of agitated voices urged departing carriages or trains. She always had a book in her hand and she was never busy; she would put it down and her arms would open to enclose any human being, but particularly a child, who needed a refuge there; what she gave was affection pure and simple, deliberately free from wear and tear of understanding or advice. She did this because she believed in affection as the panacea for all the evil in the world, and the essence of this simple love has wound itself in my memory with her scent of eau-de-cologne, and her blonde lace, and the wide silk folds and bits of warm satin that made up the black friendly labyrinth of her gowns. There one nestled for hours while she told stories. The book of Genesis, myths of Greece, the Siegfried sagas, the Seven Kings of Rome, Tasso, Dante, Goethe, came to me in this good way, not arid noises from a mechanical cavern, or black and white deserts of print, but warm with the person of the teller, modulated with the inflections of a voice that meant safety and kindness, so that the childhood of the world merged with my own and lies there entranced in the same afternoon light that melted into twilight, and gradually dimmed the ivory face and left the voice almost alone to call up pageant after pageant, while one fondled the small hands, so soft and old, whose rings had taken the shape of the fingers and lost their lustre through more than half a century of wear.

On several occasions in previous Crackers I have made a little innocent fun of Henry James; so it's only fair that I should now quote a passage from him in pure admiration. It strikes me as an astonishing prophecy, and comes from a letter that he wrote to his brother William from London – where he had just settled – in 1877:

I have a sort of feeling that if we are to see the *déchéance* of England it is inevitable, and will come to pass somewhat in this way. She will push further and further her non-fighting and keeping-out-of-scrapes policy, until contemptuous Europe, growing audacious with impunity, shall put upon her some supreme and unendurable affront. Then – too late – she will rise ferociously and plunge clumsily and unpreparedly into war. She will be worsted and laid on her back – and when she is laid on her back will exhibit – in her colossal wealth and pluck – an unprecedented power of resistance. But she will never really recover as a European power.

Where, in what bubbly land, below
  What rosy horizon dwells today
That worthy man Monsieur Cliquot
  Whose widow has made the world so gay?
  Where now is Mr Tanqueray?
Where might the King of Sheba be
  (Whose wife stopped dreadfully long away)?
Mais où sont messieurs les maris?

Say, where did Mr Beeton go
  With rubicund nose and whiskers grey
To dream of dumplings long ago,
  Of syllabubs, soups and *entremets*?
  In what dim isle did Twankey lay
His aching head? What murmuring sea
  Lulls him after the life-long fray?
Mais où sont messieurs les maris?

How Mr Grundy's cheeks may glow
  By a bathing-pool where lovelies play,
I guess, but shall I ever know?
  Where – if it comes to that, *who*, pray –
  Is Mr Masham? Sévigné
And Mr Siddons and Zebedee
  And Gamp and Hemans, where are they?
Mais où sont messieurs les maris?

Envoi

Princesses all, beneath your sway
  In this brave world they bowed the knee;
Libertine airs in Elysium say
Mais où sont messieurs les maris?

C. S. Lewis

Some years ago my friend John Jolliffe sent me this splendid extract from the Diary of Benjamin Robert Haydon, April 1813:

I dined on Friday last with a man of Genius, William Hazlitt. His child was to be christened, and I was desired to be there punctually at four. At four I came, but he was out! his wife ill by the fire, nothing ready, and all wearing the appearance of neglect and indifference. At last home he came, the cloth began to cover the table, and there followed a plate with a dozen large, waxen, cold, clayey, slaty potatoes. Down they were set, and down we sat also: a young mathematician, who whenever he spoke, jerked up one side of his mouth, and closed an eye as if seized with a paralytic affliction, thus [a sketch]; an old Lady of Genius with torn ruffles; his Wife in an influenza, thin, pale and spitty; and his chubby child, squalling, obstinate, and half-cleaned. After waiting a little, all looking forlornly at the potatoes for fear they might be the chief dish, in issued a bit of overdone beef, burnt, toppling about on seven or eight corners, with a great bone sticking out like a battering ram; the great difficulty was to make it stand upright! but the greater to discover a *cuttable* piece, for all was jagged, jutting, and irregular. Like a true Genius he forgot to go for a Parson to christen his child, till it was so late that every Parson was out or occupied, so his child was not christened. I soon retired, for tho' beastliness & indifference to the common comforts of life may amuse for a time, they soon weary & disgust those who prefer attention and cleanliness.

Two wonderful passages from Paradise Lost:

Now came still Evening on, and Twilight gray
Had in her sober Liverie all things clad;
Silence accompanied, for Beast and Bird,
They to thir grassie Couch, these to their Nests
Were slunk, all but the wakeful Nightingale;
She all night long her amorous descant sung;
Silence was pleas'd: now glow'd the Firmament
With living Saphirs: Hesperus that led
The starrie Host, rode brightest, till the Moon
Rising in clouded Majestie, at length
Apparent Queen unvailed her peerless light,
And o'er the dark her Silver Mantle threw.

Book IV

. . . and now went forth the Morn
Such as in highest Heav'n, arrayed in Gold
Empyreal, from before her vanisht Night,
Shot through with orient Beams: when all the Plain
Coverd with thick embattled Squadrons bright,
Chariots and flaming Armes, and fierie Steeds
Reflecting blaze on blaze, first met his view.

Book VI

Once in June, after sunset, very late and still, he leaned over the gate of his garden and talked to me of Shakespeare's lyrics, and of the fragility of loveliness in life. The air was full of the scent of his own flowers, and the wisdom of his speech, genial yet deep, seemed part of the beauty of the summer night.

Neville Cardus
(of Samuel Langford)

The following palindromic dialogue between Adam and Eve by J. A. Lindon appeared in the Scientific American *of February 1976, quoted by Martin Gardner in his regular feature on 'Mathematical Recreations':*

A: Madam –
E: Oh, who –
A: (No girl-rig on!)
E: Heh?
A: Madam, I'm Adam.
E: Name of a foe-man?
A: O stone me! Not so.
E: Mad. A maid I am, Adam.
A: Pure, eh? Called Ella? Cheer up.
E: Eve, not Ella. Brat-star ballet on? *Eve.*
A: Eve?
E: Eve, maiden name. Both sad in Eden? I dash to be manned. I am Eve.
A: Eve. Drowsy baby's word. Eve.
E: Mad! A gift. I fit fig, Adam . . .
A: On, hostess? Ugh! Gussets? Oh no!
E: ???
A: Sleepy baby peels.
E: Wolf! Low!
A: Wolf? Fun, so snuff 'low'.
E: Yes, low! Yes, nil on, no linsey-wolsey!
A: Madam, I'm Adam. Named under a ban, a bared nude man – Aha!
E: Mad Adam!
A: Mmmmmmmmm!
E: Mmmmmmmmm!
A: Even in Eden I win Eden in Eve.
E: Pure woman in Eden, I win Eden in – a mower-up!
A: Mmmmmmmmm!
E: Adam, I'm Ada!
A: Miss, I'm Cain, a monomaniac. Miss, I'm –
E: No, son.
A: Name's Abel, a male base man. Miss, I'm –
E: No, son.
A: Name's Abel, a male base man.
E: Name not so, O stone man!
A: Mad as it is, it is Adam.
E: I'm a Madam, Adam, am I?
A: Eve?
E: Eve mine. Denied, a jade in Eden, I'm Eve.
A: No fig. (Nor wrong if on!)
E: ???
A: A daffodil I doff, Ada.
E: 'Tis a – what – ah, was it –
A: Sun ever! A bare Venus . . .
E: 'S pity! So red, ungirt, rig-nude, rosy tips . . .
A: Eve is a sieve!
E: Tut, tut!
A: Now a see-saw on . . .
E: On me? (O poem!) No!
A: Aha!
E: I won't! O not now, I –
A: Aha!
E: No! O God, I – (Fit if I do?) *Go on.*
A: Hrrrrrh!
E: Wow! Ow!
A: Sores? (Alas, Eros!)
E: No, none. My hero! More hymen, on, on . . .
A: Hrrrrrrrrrrrrrrrrrh!
E: Revolting is error. Resign it, lover.
A: No, not now I won't. On, on . . .
E: Rise sir.
A: Dewy dale, cinema-game . . . Nice lady wed?
E: Marry an Ayr ram!
A: Rail on, O liar!
E: Live devil!
A: Diamond-eyed no-maid!
Both: Mmmmmmmmmmmmm!
A: Diamond-eyed no-maid!
Both: Mmmmmmmmmmmmm!

It was Hester up in Chester, it was Jenny down in Kent;
Up and down the motorways, the same where'er he went.
In Luton it was Sally, quite the nicest of the bunch,
But down on his expenses they were petrol, oil and lunch.

Anon.

Two short poems that somehow came out not quite as the authors had intended:

Why leapest thou,
Why leapest thou,
So high within my breast?
Oh stay thee now,
Oh stay thee now,
Thou little bounder, rest.

Ruskin

Ages and ages, returning at intervals
Undestroyed, wandering, immortal,
Lusty, phallic, with the potent original
Loins, perfectly sweet.

Walt Whitman,
Leaves of Grass

J. L. Motley's famous paragraph on William the Silent, assassinated on Tuesday 10 July, 1584:

He went through life bearing the load of a people's sorrows upon his shoulder with a smiling face. Their name was the last word upon his lips, save the simple affirmative with which the soldier who had been battling for the right all his lifetime commended his soul in dying 'to his great captain, Christ'. The people were grateful and affectionate, for they trusted the character of their 'Father William' and not all the clouds which calumny could collect ever dimmed to their eyes the radiance of that lofty mind to which they were accustomed, in their darkest calamities, to look for light. As long as he lived he was the guiding-star of a whole brave nation, and when he died the little children cried in the streets.

C. V. Wedgwood goes still further:

Few statesmen in any period, none in his own, cared so deeply for the ordinary comfort and the trivial happiness of the thousands of individuals who are the people. He neither idealized nor overestimated them and he knew that they were often wrong, for what political education had they yet had? But he believed in them, not merely as a theoretical concept, but as individuals, as men. Therein lay the secret of the profound and enduring love between him and them. Wise, wary, slow to judge and slow to act, patient, stubborn and undiscouraged, no other man could have sustained so difficult a cause for so long, could have opposed with so little sacrifice of public right the concentrated power of a government which disregarded it. He respected in all men what he wished to have respected in himself, the right to an opinion.

'The wisest, gentlest and bravest man who ever led a nation', he is one of that small band of statesmen whose service to humanity is greater than their service to their time or their people . . . Such men, in whatever walk of life, in whatever chapter of fame, mystic or saint, scientist or doctor, poet or philosopher or even – but how rarely – soldier or statesman, exist to shame the cynic, and to renew the faith of humanity in itself.

Mrs Margaret Dawlings has kindly sent me the following letter to the London North Western Railway Company from one of its passengers:

Botanic Gardens, Oxford

15 June 1865

Sir,

On the 13th I took a ticket at Carlisle for Birmingham on the way to Oxford and when we arrived at Preston the recollections I had of Birmingham seven years ago made me conclude that we were at Birmingham. I there applied for a fresh ticket to Oxford and got one to Bletchley. On discovering my mistake I thought best to go to Birmingham, pay for another ticket from there to Bletchley and apply to you with the ticket I already possessed to be refunded and as I paid twice for the distance between Preston and Bletchley I trust you will have the goodness to give me the money back.

In excuse for my blunder I have only to say that I feel very much confused in travelling by railway as I suppose you might be if travelling in Africa where I should be at home.

I got bewildered at Wolverhampton and spent the night there and next day was told that my Bletchley ticket was out of date. I have no one to blame but myself and if you can refund the money on the ground that I paid for the distance between Preston and Bletchley twice and only travelled over it once, you will oblige.

Yours faithfully,

David Livingstone.

I enclose the tickets for your consideration and will feel obliged by an answer to Dr Livingstone, at John Murray's, 50 Albemarle Street, London.

From Harrap's Guide de Conversation, Français–Anglais, *by 'Lexus', 1988:*

Problèmes

– Je n'ai pas assez d'argent
aïe done-te Hève inafe meuni

– Je suis tombé en panne
aï've brôkeune daoune

– La lumière ne marche pas dans ma chambre
Ze laïtse âne-te ouerkine ine maï roume

– L'ascenseur est en panne
Ze lifte ize steuke

– Je ne comprends rien
aïe cânte eune-deurstènde a sine-guele oueurde

– La chasse d'eau ne marche pas
Ze toïlète ouone-te fleuche

– Il n'y a pas de bonde pour la baignoire
Zèrze nö pleugue ine Ze bathe

– Il n'y a pas d'eau chaude
Zèrze nô Hote ouateu

– Il n'y a plus de papier hygiénique
Zèrze nô toïlète pépeu lèfte

– Je suis désolé, j'ai cassé le/la . . .
aïme èfréde aïve axidèntali brôkeune Ze . . .

– Cet homme me suit depuis un moment
Zisse mane Hèze bine foloïne mi

– J'ai été attaqué
aïve bine meugde.

A single flow'r he sent me since we met,
All tenderly his messenger he chose.
Deep-hearted, pure, with scented dew still wet,
   One perfect rose.

I knew the language of the floweret,
'My fragile leaves,' it said, 'his heart enclose.'
Love long has taken, for its amulet
   One perfect rose.

Why is it no one ever sent me yet
One perfect limousine, do you suppose?
Ah no, it's always just my luck to get
   One perfect rose.

                                        Dorothy Parker

Bonus

A hotel correspondence, passed to me by Judith Flanders:

Dear Maid,

Please do not leave any more of those little bars of soap in my bathroom, since I have brought my own bath-sized Dial. Please remove the six unopened little bars from the shelf under the medicine chest and another three in the shower soapdish.

Thank you, S. Berman

Dear Room 635,

I am not your regular maid. She will be back tomorrow, Thursday, from her day off. I took the three hotel soaps out of the shower soapdish as you requested. The six bars on your shelf I took out of your way and put on top of your Kleenex dispenser in case you should change your mind. This leaves only the three bars I left today; my instructions from the management are to leave three daily. I hope this is satisfactory.

Kathy, Relief Maid

Dear Maid,

I hope you are my regular maid. Apparently Kathy did not tell you of my note to her concerning the little bars of soap. When I got back to my room this evening I found you had added three little Camays to the shelf under my medicine cabinet. I am going to be here in the hotel for two weeks and have brought my own bath-size Dial, so I won't need those six little Camays which are on the shelf. They are in my way when shaving, brushing teeth, etc. Please remove them.

S. Berman

Dear Mr Berman,

My day off was last We. so the relief maid left three hotel soaps, which we are instructed by the management. I took the six soaps, which were in your way on the shelf, and put them in the soapdish where your Dial was. I put the Dial in the medicine cabinet. I didn't remove the three complimentary soaps which are always placed inside the medicine cabinet for all new check-ins and which you did not object to last Monday. Please, let me know if I can be of further assistance.

Your regular maid, Dotty

Dear Mr Berman,

The assistant manager, Mr Kensedder, informed me this a.m. that you called him last evening and said you were unhappy with your maid service. I have assigned a new girl to your room. I hope you will accept my apologies for any past inconvenience. If you have any future complaints, please contact me so I can give it my personal attention. Call extension 1108 between 8 a.m. and 5 p.m. Thank you.

Elaine Carmen, Housekeeper

Dear Miss Carmen,

It is impossible to contact you by phone since I leave the hotel for business at 7.45 a.m. and don't get back before 5.30 or 6 p.m. That's the reason I called Mr Kensedder last night. You were already off duty. I only asked Mr Kensedder if he could do anything about those little bars of soap. The new maid you assigned me must have thought I was a new check-in today, since she left another three bars of hotel soap in my medicine cabinet, together with her regular delivery of three bars on the bathroom shelf. In just five days I have accumulated twenty-four little bars of soap. Why are you doing this to me?

S. Berman

Dear Mr Berman,

Your maid, Kathy, has been instructed to stop delivering soap to your room and remove the extra soaps. If I can be of further assistance, please call extension 1108 between 8 a.m. and 5 p.m. Thank you.

Elaine Carmen, Housekeeper

Dear Mr Kensedder,

My bath-sized Dial is missing. Every bar of soap was taken from my room including my own bath-sized Dial. I came in late last night and had to call the bell-hop to bring me four little Cashmere Bouquets.

S. Berman

Dear Mr Berman,

I have informed our housekeeper, Elaine Carmen, of your soap problem. I cannot understand why there was no soap in your room since our maids are instructed to leave three bars of soap each time they come to service a room. The situation will be rectified immediately. Please accept my apologies for the inconvenience.

Martin L. Kensedder
Assistant Manager

Dear Mrs Carmen,

Who the hell left fifty-four little bars of Camay in my room? I came in last night and found fifty-four little bars of soap. I want my one damn bar of bath-sized Dial. Do you realize I have fifty-four bars of soap in here. All I want is my bath-sized Dial. Please give back my bath-sized Dial.

S. Berman

Dear Mr Berman,

You complained of too much soap in your room so I had them removed. Then you complained to Mr Kensedder that all your soap was missing so I personally returned them. The twenty-four Camays which had been taken and the three Camays you are supposed to receive daily. I don't know anything about the Cashmere Bouquets. Obviously your maid, Kathy, did not know I had returned your soaps so she also brought twenty-four Camays plus the three daily Camays. I don't know where you got the idea this hotel issues bath-sized Dial. I was able to locate some bath-sized Ivory which I left in your room.

Elaine Carmen, Housekeeper

Dear Mrs Carmen,

Just a short note to bring you up to date on my latest soap inventory. As of today I possess:

On shelf under medicine cabinet – 18 Camay in 4 stacks of 4 and 1 stack of 2

On Kleenex dispenser – 11 Camay in 2 stacks of 4 and 1 stack of 3

On bedroom dresser – 1 stack of 3 Cashmere Bouquet, 1 stack of 4 hotel-size Ivory and 8 Camay in 2 stacks of 4

Inside medicine cabinet – 14 Camay in 3 stacks of 4 and 1 stack of 2

In shower soapdish – 6 Camay, very moist

On north-east corner of tub – 1 Cashmere Bouquet, slightly used

On north-west corner of tub – 6 Camay in 2 stacks of 3

Please ask Kathy when she services my room to make sure the stacks are neatly piled and dusted. Also, please advise her that stacks of more than four have a tendency to tip. May I suggest that my bedroom windowsill is not in use and will make an excellent spot for future soap deliveries.

One more item. I have purchased another bar of bath-sized Dial, which I am keeping in the hotel vault to avoid further misunderstandings.

S. Berman

A
Christmas
Cracker

1994

In the Bodleian Library at Oxford (Arch.F.c.4a.f.54) is a sheet of Privy Council notes in the handwritings of Charles II and his High Chancellor, Lord Clarendon. It reads as follows:

KING: I would willingly make a visite to my sister at Tunbridge for a night or two at farthest, when do you thinke I can best spare that time?

CLARENDON: I know no reason why you may not for such a tyme, (2 nights) go the next weeke, about Wensday, or Thursday, and returne tyme enough for the adiournement, which yett ought to be the weeke followinge. I suppose you will goe with a light Trayne.

KING: I intend to take nothing but my night bag.

CLARENDON: Yet, you will not goe without 40 or 50 horses!

KING: I counte that parte of my night bag.

[The biographer of King George V, Kenneth Rose, has since told me that when, in 1935, the King went down to stay with the Duke of Devonshire at Compton Place for a rest before his Silver Jubilee, he said it would be 'a quiet interlude'. He took 45 servants.]

George Eliot's Middlemarch *has suddenly – thanks to its translation to television – become a national bestseller. It has one of the best endings of any book I know, describing the life of Dorothea after the story ends:*

> Her finely-touched spirit had still its fine issues, though they were not widely visible. Her full nature, like that river of which Cyrus broke the strength, spent itself in channels which had no great name on the earth. But the effect of her being on those around her was incalculably diffusive: for the growing good of the world is partly dependent on unhistoric acts; and that things are not so ill with you and me as they might have been, is half owing to the number who lived faithfully a hidden life, and rest in unvisited tombs.

I had to look up the bit about Cyrus. According to Dr Lemprière, he captured Babylon by 'drying' – by which the good doctor presumably means diverting – 'the channels of the Euphrates, and marching his troops through the bed of the river, while the people were celebrating a grand festival'.

A fine old English Music Hall song from the first years of the twentieth century:

The War, the War, the dreadful War
Has turned my wife insane.
From Kruger to Majuba
She's the Transvaal on the brain.
So when to christen our first babe
Last Sunday week we tried,
The parson said: 'What's this child's name?'
And my old girl replied:

Chorus   The baby's name is –
Kitchener Carrington Methuen Kekewich
White Cronje Plumer Powell
Majuba Gatacre Warren Colenso
Kruger Capetown Mafeking French
Kimberley Ladysmith Bobs
Union Jack Fighting Mack Lyddite Pretoria Bloggs.

The parson said: 'This name I can't
Upon an infant plop!'
But my wife broke his roaring Meg
And smashed his Spion Kop.
She kicked his mounted infantry
Till his Bloemfontein was sore,
Then she did a flanking movement
And she shouted out once more:

Chorus   The baby's name is –
Kitchener Carrington Methuen Kekewich
White Cronje Plumer Powell
Majuba Gatacre Warren Colenso
Kruger Capetown Mafeking French
Kimberley Ladysmith Bobs
Union Jack Fighting Mack Lyddite Pretoria Bloggs.

As no man be very miserable that is master of a *Garden here*; so will no man ever be happy who is not sure of a *Garden hereafter*. . . where the first Adam fell, the second rose.

I read this inscription engraved on a pedestal in the glorious garden of Mrs Rosemary Verey at Barnsley, Gloucestershire, on 20 July 1986. That same afternoon Mrs Verey also showed me a letter she had recently received from a Japanese visitor. It enclosed a ginger root, and ran:

> Mrs Rosemary Verey
> Thankyou very much for everything.
> Today's morning.
> I found other present for you to my Seiko in my bag.
> (oh my God, I have mistake once more . . .)
> That is Ginger, Zingiher officinale.
> It is living now. happy!
> I must send to you in haste!
> Thank you very much for bottle of my heart.
>
> Naotaka Hirota,
27 June 1986

I stole through the dungeons while everyone slept,
Till I came to the place where the monster was kept;
There, locked in the arms of the Giant Baboon,
Rigid and smiling, lay . . . MRS RAVOON.

I climbed the church tower in the first morning sun,
And 'twas midday at least ere my journey was done;
But the clock never sounded the last stroke of noon,
For there from the clapper swung . . . MRS RAVOON.

I hauled in the line and I took my first look
At the half-eaten horror that hung from the hook:
I had dragged from the depths of the limpid lagoon
The luminous body of . . . MRS RAVOON.

I fled in the dark through the lightning and thunder,
And there, as a flash split the darkness asunder,
Chewing a rat's tail and mumbling a rune,
Mad in the moat squatted . . . MRS RAVOON.

I stood by the waters so green and so thick,
And I stirred at the scum with my old withered stick,
When there rose from the ooze like a floating balloon
The bloated cadaver of . . . MRS RAVOON.

Facing the fens, I looked back from the shore,
Where all had been empty a moment before;
And there, by the light of the Lincolnshire moon,
Immense on the marshes stood . . . MRS RAVOON.

Mrs Ravoon was first introduced to me by Linda Kelly, though she was actually the creation of the late Paul Dehn; she made her début in his book The Fern on the Rock. *After that she was unstoppable: what Dehn described as 'Ravoon sightings' continued. Sometimes they were his own, as in*

> As a whaler, I knew I was meeting my match,
> But I heaved on the rope and I landed my catch;
> Transfixed by the spike of the bloody harpoon,
> Nodding and smiling, twitched . . . MRS RAVOON.

and sometimes those of others, long after his death in 1976. Two recent examples:

A torch flickered, deep in the Valley of Kings:
'I see', whispered Carter, 'oh, wonderful things!'
'Do you think,' gasped Carnarvon, 'it's Tutankhamun?'
Then it sat up and leered: it was . . . MRS RAVOON.

and

Below the salt Channel they're drinking champagne
And ministers jostle to board the first train.
Emergency bells ring in French and Walloon,
For there on the buffers squats . . . MRS RAVOON.

From Julian Mitchell comes this passage from The Compleat Servant-Maid, or Young Maiden's Tutor, *second edition, 1680:*

In cutting up small birds it is proper to say thigh them, as THIGH that Woodcock, THIGH that Pigeon: but as to the others say, MINCE that Plover, WING that Quail, and WING that Partridge, ALLAY that Pheasant, UNTACK that Curlew, UNJOINT that Bittern, DIS-FIGURE that Peacock, DISPLAY that Crane, DISMEMBER that Hern, UNBRACE that Mallard, FRUST that Chicken, SPOYL that Hen, SAWCE that Capon, LIFT that Swan, REER that Goose, TIRE that Egg: as to the flesh of beasts, UNLACE that Coney, BREAK that Deer, LEACH that Brawn.

[At this point something rather embarrassing happened: I included an item which had already appeared in an earlier Cracker, that of 1979. For the sake of completeness, however, I suppose it had better go in again.]

In his book The Cecils of Hatfield House, *Lord David Cecil painted an unforgettable portrait of his grandfather, Lord Salisbury, who was Prime Minister of England, with two short interruptions, between 1885 and 1902:*

All his life my grandfather retained his interest in science, and he liked to introduce recent scientific innovations into his home. Hatfield was one of the first places to have an inter-communicating telephone. My grandfather enjoyed testing its efficiency, by reciting nursery rhymes down it. Unsuspecting visitors, sitting as they thought alone, would be alarmed to hear, emerging from a mysterious instrument on a neighbouring table, the spectral voice of the Prime Minister intoning:

> Hey diddle diddle,
> The cat and the fiddle . . .

My grandfather was also a pioneer in installing electric light. This was even more alarming to the guests than the telephone. The naked uninsulated wires stretched on the ceiling of the Long Gallery would suddenly burst into flames. My grandfather, conversing below, would look up; he or his sons would nonchalantly toss up a cushion to put the flames out and then resume their conversation.

'During the German Emperor's recent visit to Brussels,' wrote the Daily Mail, 'Baron de Haulleville, Director of the Congo Museum, was presented to His Majesty. The Kaiser spoke at length with the Baron in French, German and English'. Harry Graham imagined the conversation:

'Guten Morgen, mon ami!
  Heute ist es schönes Wetter!
Charmé de vous voir ici!
  Never saw you looking better!

'Hoffentlich que la Baronne
  So entzückend et so pleasant,
Ist in Brussels cet automne.
  Combien wünsch' ich she were present!

'Und die Kinder, how are they?
  Ont-ils eu la rougeole lately?
Sind sie avec vous today?
  J'aimerais les treffen greatly.

'Ich muss chercher mon hôtel.
  What a charming Schwätzerei, sir!
Lebe wohl! Adieu! Farewell!
  Vive le Congo! Hoch der Kaiser!'

In California, car owners are allowed to select their 'personalized' licence plates, choosing any combination of letters and figures or of letters only. I read in an article by Ben Macintyre in The Times of the recent publication of a book, Literary Licence, by one Daniel Nussbaum, who retells the tales of classical mythology using only those combinations he has actually seen. Now, to my delight, I have acquired a copy. Here is Mr Nussbaum's rendering of Sophocles' Oedipus Rex:

ONCEPON ATIME LONG AGO IN THEBES IMKING. OEDIPUS DAKING. LVMYMRS. LVMYKIDS. THEBENS THINK OEDDY ISCOOL. NOPROBS. OKAY MAYBE THEREZZ 1LITL1. MOTHER WHERERU? WHEREAT MYDAD? NOCALLZ NEVER. HAVENOT ACLUE. INMYMIND IWNDER WHOAMI? I MUST FINDEM.

JO MYWIFE GOES: 'OED DONT USEE? WERHAPPI NOW LET-ITBE.' IGO: 'NOWAY. IAMBOSS. DONTU TELLME MY LIFE. I NEED MYMOM. II WILLL FINDHER. FIND BOTHOF THEM.'

SOI START SEEKING DATRUTH ABOUT WHO IAM. ITGOEZ ULTRAAA SLOWE. THE SPHYNXS RIDDLE WAS ACINCH BUT NOTTHIZ.

SUDNLEE WEHEAR SHOCKING NEWS. WHEN IWASA TINY1 THISGR8 4SEER SED IWOOD OFF MY ROYAL OLDMAN THEN MAREE MYMAMA. SICKO RUBBISH, NESTPAS? WHOWHO COUDBE SOGONE? STIL MOMNDAD SENT MEEEEE A WAY. MEE ABABI AWAAAY.

NOWWWWW GETTTHIZ. MANY MOONS GOBY. I MEET THIS-GUY ONATRIP. WEDOO RUMBLE. WHOKNEW? I LEFTMY POP ONE DEDMAN.

UGET DATOTO. MAJR TSURIS. JOJO MYHONEE, MYSQEEZ, MYLAMBY, MIAMOR. MYCUTEE. JOJOY IZZ MYMOMMY.

YEGODS WHYMEE? YMEYYME? LIFSUX. IAMBAD, IAMBADD, IMSOBAD. STOPNOW THISS HEDAKE. THIS FLESH DUZ STINK. ITZ 2MUCH PAYNE 4oNE2C. TAKEGOD MYEYES! AIEEEEE!

From What's On? – Wiltshire Wildlife Week, *published by the Wiltshire Trust for Nature Conservation, 14–22 June 1991:*

On Sunday June 2 the Pewsey Group are putting together an unusual combination of attractions, to be staged on the grassy slopes of Martinsell. The centrepiece will be a game of COWPAT ROULETTE. A field at the base of the hill will be marked out in squares, and participants will stake money on one or more squares. Then a cow is led in and eventually performs on whatever square it chooses to make the winning square. If necessary, a further cow can be introduced for a further round. The field is clearly visible from the flat area above, where there will be a marquee. It can also be seen from the whole path to the summit of Martinsell so if people like to walk to the top of the hill, they can do so while keeping an eye on the cow and their fortunes below. Also the time can be filled at a barbecue, stalls for plants and produce, or at a Wiltshire wine tasting.

My lyre I tune, my voice I raise;
　　But with my numbers mix my sighs:
And while I sing Euphelia's praise,
　　I fix my soul on Chloe's eyes.

Fair Chloe blushed: Euphelia frowned:
　　I sang, and gazed: I play'd, and trembled:
And Venus to the Loves around
　　Remark'd, how ill we all dissembled.

Matthew Prior

Uncle Matthew went with Aunt Sadie and Linda on one occasion to a Shakespeare play, *Romeo and Juliet*. It was not a success. He cried copiously, and went into a furious rage because it ended badly. 'All the fault of that damned padre,' he kept saying on the way home, still wiping his eyes. 'That fella, what's 'is name, Romeo, might have known a blasted papist would mess up the whole thing. Silly old nurse too, I bet she was an RC, dismal old bitch.'

Nancy Mitford,
The Pursuit of Love

Two sonnets by Edna St Vincent Millay:

> What lips my lips have kissed, and where, and why,
> I have forgotten, and what arms have lain
> Under my head till morning; but the rain
> Is full of ghosts tonight, that tap and sigh
> Upon the glass and listen for reply,
> And in my heart there stirs a quiet pain
> For unremembered lads that not again
> Will turn to me at midnight with a cry.
> Thus in the winter stands the lonely tree,
> Nor knows what birds have vanished one by one,
> Yet knows its boughs more silent than before:
> I cannot say what loves have come and gone,
> I only know that summer sang in me
> A little while, that in me sings no more.

> Love is not all: it is not meat or drink
> Nor slumber, nor a roof against the rain;
> Nor yet a floating spar to men that sink
> And rise and sink and rise and sink again;
> Love cannot fill the thickened lung with breath,
> Nor clean the blood, nor set the fractured bone;
> Yet many a man is making friends with death
> Even as I speak, for lack of love alone.
> It may well be that in a difficult hour,
> Pinned down by pain and moaning for release,
> Or nagged by want past resolution's power,
> I might be driven to sell your love for peace,
> Or trade the memory of this night for food.
> It may well be. I do not think I would.

[Dorothy Parker wrote:

We all wandered in after Miss Millay. We were all being dashing and gallant, declaring that we weren't virgins whether we were or not. Beautiful as she was, Miss Millay did a great deal of harm with her double-burning candles . . . made poetry seem so easy that we could all do it. But, of course, we couldn't.

How strange that Miss Millay should not be represented in either the Oxford Book of English, *or even the* Oxford Book of American, *Verse.]*

An announcement in the Cork Examiner:

Donnachie's Bar, Cobh. Due to the sad death of Paddy, the Bar, to all intents and purposes, will remain closed during our grief; but so as not to inconvenience our esteemed customers, the door will remain ajar. 'Tis what Paddy wanted. Thank you. The Donnachie family.

The aged sire unto the matron gave
A liquor far more precious than gold,
Of which the secret virtue to unfold:
It would not only cause a strong erection,
But, working on the mind, procure affection.

*These refreshingly awful lines are taken from 'Leoline and Syranus', by Sir Francis
Kynaston, 1642. When one has read them, the fact that Kynaston was tutor to the
future Charles II seems to assume a new significance.*

*Here are three equally atrocious passages: first, from 'Love's Complaint', by
Thomas Carew:*

I do not love thee for that belly,
Sleek as satin, soft as jelly . . .

second, from 'Nereides' (1732), by the charmingly named William Diaper:

I hate the skittish Fair, that flies when woo'd
Like fearful Tunnys, when by Sharks pursued.

*and finally (thanks to my friend Brian Young) a perfectly dreadful quatrain
addressed to George II by the Rev. Laurence Eusden – who was, believe it or not,
Poet Laureate from 1718 till his death in 1730:*

Hail, mighty Monarch! whom desert alone
Would, without birthright, raise up to the throne;
Thy virtues shine particularly nice,
Ungloomed with a confinity to vice.

The present is a fleeting moment, the past is no more; and our prospect of futurity is dark and doubtful. This day may *possibly* be my last: but the laws of probability, so true in general, so fallacious in particular, still allow about fifteen years. I shall soon enter into the period which, as the most agreeable of his long life, was selected by the judgement and experience of the sage Fontenelle. His choice is approved by the eloquent historian of nature, who fixes our moral happiness to the mature season in which our passions are supposed to be calmed, our desires fulfilled, our ambition satisfied, our fame and fortune established on a solid basis. In private conversation, that great and amiable man added the weight of his own experience; and this autumnal felicity might be exemplified in the lives of Voltaire, Hume and many other men of letters. I am far more inclined to embrace than to dispute this comfortable doctrine. I will not suppose any premature decay of the mind or body; but I must reluctantly observe that two causes, the abbreviation of time, and the failure of hope, will always tinge with a brown shade the evening of life.

The proportion of a part to the whole is the only standard by which we can measure the length of our existence. At the age of twenty, one year is a tenth perhaps of the time which has elapsed within our consciousness and memory; at the age of fifty it is no more than a fortieth, and this relative value continues to decrease till the last sands are shaken by the hand of death. This reasoning may seem metaphysical; but on a trial it will be found satisfactory and just. The warm desires, the long expectations of youth, are founded on the ignorance of themselves and of the world: they are gradually damped by time and experience, by disappointment or possession; and after the middle season the crowd must be content to remain at the foot of the mountain; while the few who have climbed the summit aspire to descend or expect to fall. In old age, the consolation of hope is reserved for the tenderness of parents, who commence a new life in their children; the faith of enthusiasts, who sing Hallelujahs above the clouds; and the vanity of authors, who presume the immortality of their name and writings.

Thus he ended his account of his life, adding, according to his usual fashion, the place and date: 'Lausanne, March 2: 1791'. He was at the time just eight weeks short of his fifty-fourth birthday.

Horace Walpole, as might have been expected, took the matter rather more lightly:

Old age is no such uncomfortable thing, if one gives oneself up to it with a good grace, and don't drag it about

> To midnight dances and the public show.

If one stays quietly in one's own house in the country, and cares for nothing but oneself, scolds one's servants, condemns everything that is new, and recollects how charming a thousand things were formerly that were very disagreeable, one gets over the winters very well, and the summers get over themselves.

EPITAPH FOR A TIMID LADY

When I was born a happy child,
The waves ahead looked sweet and wild.
I lie beneath the final sheet
Who never found them wild or sweet.
I did not wish to wet my feet.

Frances Cornford

The Reverend Paul Kingdon, the scholar priest who has died aged 82, was well known in Oxford in the 1930s but never fulfilled his early promise.

Although a Fellow of Exeter College, Oxford, from 1933 to 1945, he had no vocation as a teacher. He was relentless in the pursuit of arcane detail and lectured in terms so obscure that few of his students could understand him.

Sadly, he fared little better as a parish priest. He had a remarkable capacity for creating misunderstanding and often left a trail of havoc behind him . . .

Henry Paul Kingdon was born in 1907 and was educated at Corpus Christi College, Oxford, where he just missed a double first in Greats. He took the Diploma in Theology with distinction and then studied at Tübingen, where he was introduced to the liberal German theologians of the time . . .

At the end of the 1939–45 War, the College presented Kingdon to the living of Somerford in Wiltshire. In 1951 he returned to teaching, at King Alfred's College, Winchester. He was not a success there and left in 1956.

Kingdon then became Vicar of Chewton Mendip, near Bath, and was also appointed as a lecturer at Wells Theological College. He was quite unfitted for both these posts, the second of which lasted no more than a fortnight.

Fortunately, he inherited enough money to retire in 1964, to Almondsbury in Bristol, where, relieved of the burden of parochial responsibility, he exercised a much appreciated personal ministry as an honorary curate of the parish church.

His wife, Joan, predeceased him.

Si vous me disiez que la terre
  A tant tourner vous offensa,
  Je lui dépêcherais Pança:
Vous la verriez fixe et se taire.

Si vous me disiez que l'ennui
  Vous vient du ciel trop fleuri d'astres,
  Déchirant les divins cadastres,
Je faucherais d'un coup la nuit.

Si vous me disiez que l'espace
  Ainsi vide ne vous plaît point,
  Chevalier dieu, la lance au point,
J'étoilerais le vent qui passe.

Mais si vous disiez que mon sang
  Est plus à moi qu'à vous, ma Dame,
  Je blêmirais dessous le blâme
Et je mourrais, vous bénissant.

*I've always loved this little 'chanson romanesque' by Paul Morand. Since some
Cracker-readers have chided me for not giving translations of French items, here
is a not very satisfactory attempt at one:*

DON QUIXOTE TO DULCINEA

If, you said, it was your will
  That Earth itself should cease to spin,
  I'd send my Sancho Panza in,
And you would find it quiet and still.

And if, you said, it made you choke
  To see the sky so full of stars,
  I'd spit at heaven's registrars
And slice the lot off at a stroke.

And if, you said, it failed to please –
  This void we'd made by some mischance –
  Then, knight divine with ready lance,
I'd strew with stars the passing breeze.

> But if, you said, 'Your life and breath
>   Are yours, not mine' – then should I pale,
>   And feel my heart within me fail –
> And bless you as I welcomed death.

The lines have been marvellously set to music by Ravel; but then Don Quixote has always inspired composers. There's also Massenet's opera, written for the great Russian bass Feodor Chaliapin (whose performance Massenet loathed) and – best of all for me – the 'fantastic variations on a theme of knightly character' by Richard Strauss. In 1949, Sir Thomas Beecham was recording it with the Royal Philharmonic Orchestra, with Paul Tortelier playing the solo cello. Strauss himself was present; it was only a month or two before his death on 8 September. At one moment he stopped the music and said to Tortelier: 'No, no, you play as if Quixote is still young. He is old, very old, and very sick. Play it like a memory.'

It was not until 1864 that French was included as a regular part of the Eton College curriculum. The College Chronicle *reacted with muted enthusiasm:*

So great a part of the French vocabulary consists of Latin words corrupted or disguised, that a knowledge of the latter language, we had almost said, is equivalent to a certain proficiency in the former. This being the case, would it not be manifest waste of valuable time, to devote a laborious course of tuition to that for which a dictionary and a few brains would be sufficient? But apart from these considerations, it is at least a matter of question, whether the intrinsic merits of French literature are such as to justify the sacrifice of any considerable and definite portion of time in the routine of school-work, to the study of composition in that tongue. Artificial and shallow, the productions of French authors are very generally an exact reflex of the national character. At any rate, experience has shown that it is little short of Quixotic to aim at acquiring a correct French accent except by actual intercourse with the natives, and by deriving pronunciation of words from those who use them every day of their lives.

It is for these reasons that we hope that French will not be suffered to fill too large a space in the education of the School.

Gerard Manley Hopkins was – as I was delighted to learn from my friend (and his biographer) Robert Bernard Martin – known to his intimates as 'Tunks'. This extract from his Journals is dated 22 July 1873:

Very hot, though the wind, which was south, dappled very sweetly on one's face and when I came out I seemed to put it on like a gown as a man puts on the shadow he walks into and hoods or hats himself with the shelter of a roof, a penthouse, or a copse of trees, I mean it rippled and fluttered like light linen, one could feel the folds and braids of it – and indeed a floating flag is like wind visible and what weeds are in a current; it gives it thew and fires it and bloods it in.

Among those few and select indexes worthy to be read for their own sake – one or two have already appeared in previous Crackers – is that of the superb anthology of excruciating verse by D. B. Wyndham Lewis and Charles Lee, The Stuffed Owl. *Here are a few items therefrom:*

Adam, his internal fluids, 18
Aliments, oily, their coy behaviour in the stomach, 61; tumults and
    horrors arising from their introduction, *ibid.*
Astronomy, pursuit of, inconsistent with social obligations, 230
Baker, Mr, resources of the Muse strained by his recovery, 110;
    requests Miss Hoyland to own a mutual flame, *ibid.*
Bards, dead, common objects of the sea-shore, 66
Botanist, as mountaineer, inferior to goat, 82
Cabbage, true-hearted, 22
Carrot, sluggish, 22
Charles II, his magnetic effect on the coast-line, 31
Elephant, not amphibious, 58
Feather, Cynthia's, weather forecasts based on, 23
Fire, wetness not an attribute of, 28
Frenchmen, fraudful, mix sand with sugar, 90
Heaven, system of book-keeping in, 32; vogue of Mr Purcell's music
    in, 37; unexpected grandeur of its architecture, 48; knowledge of
    languages useful in, *ibid.*; blasted, 188; haloes the only wear in, 216
Immortality, hope of, distinguishes man from silk-worm, 152
Inebriation, infantile, adjudged blameless, 96
Italy, not recommended to tourists, 125; examples of what goes on
    there, 204, 219, 221
Lee, Miss R., said to resemble a cucumber, 184
Manure, adjudged a fit subject for the Muse, 91
Mechanic, pale, exhibited in a hurry to wallow in vice, 137
Negroes, liable to worms, 91; prone to bloat, *ibid.*; their nails often
    found in Christmas puddings, 98
Pea, not self-supporting, 22
Props, required by hops, 97
Silkworm, Spartan tastes of, 150; sinks into hopeless grave, 152
Spurs, worn on bare feet by Italian brigands, 206
Thought, silent tickler of the human brain, 18
Umbrellas, their use by Highland crofters discommended, 151
Washing, cautiously recommended, 62
Woman, useful as a protection against lions, 118

How will you manage
To cross alone
The Autumn mountain,
Which was so hard to get across
Even when we went the two of us together?

Princess Dailakin
From the *Manyo Shu*, seventh century

Bonus

Some time in the 1930s, my mother's old friend Conrad Russell was invited by his distant kinsman Herbrand, 11th Duke of Bedford, to stay at Woburn Abbey. My mother explains in the second volume of her autobiography (The Light of Common Day, p. 140) that '[the Duke's] wife, "the Flying Duchess", often "flipping about the Gold Coast in her Puss Moth", one day did not return, and the old Duke, then lonely, began to invite very occasionally members of his family to Woburn. When Conrad received his summons I made him promise to leave no detail unnoted.' This is what he wrote:

Dinner was a choice of fish and a whole partridge each. No drink except inferior claret and not much of it. Nothing else. The second that I had swallowed my peach, Herbrand sprang up and we all trooped out. He read the *Evening Standard* for 1½ hours. Miss Green (companion librarian) had been reading the Flying Duchess's account of coming to my farm in her diary. She had liked it more than any she had ever seen. 'She was envious of having a house like that.' Odd! It's an ordinary sort of very small house and suits me all right. When we arrived Herbrand was wearing a white silk tie, tweed coat, dark waistcoat, gabardine trousers (much stained and frayed around the bottoms) and very thick black buttoned boots. For dinner he wore a long-tailed coat, black tie, black waistcoat. I've got a lovely bedroom, all rosebud curtains and rosebud chintz. It's the room that Papa always had at Christmas. The bathroom is huge and stinks fearfully on account of rubber flooring. Herbrand said: 'I've put you on the first floor so that you can see the birds and squirrels better.' As it's dark I can see neither.

This is how the day passed. At nine minutes to nine we are all assembled in the Canaletto room. At nine the butler knocks loudly at the door, comes in and bawls: 'Breakfast on the table, Your Grace.' Herbrand says: 'Well, shall we go to breakfast?' We all file in then. There are five men to wait on us, one for each. Everyone has their own tea or coffee pot. You help yourself to eggs and bacon. The butler takes your plate from you and carries it to your place. You walk behind him. It makes a little procession. As soon as the last person is helped he leaves the room. Herbrand eats a prodigious number of spring onions.

Glasses of milk, apples and biscuits at eleven-thirty to keep one going until lunch, which is at two. Later a comic-opera Rolls dating to 1913 picked us up. Man on box as well as driver, and the back wheels fitted with chains as if for snowy weather. Miss Green held a small butler's tray on her lap and on the tray stood a Pekinese the size of a basset hound. The tray was supported on a single leg and hitched to the front of the car by green baize straps. By this means the dog's behind is brought to within a half-inch of one's nose. There's no escape.

We called on Constance and Romola, Lord Ampthill's daughters. They were sitting indoors in immense beefeater hats and thick cloth coats with brown braid. We all talked and screamed and said the same thing over and over again for forty minutes. Lunch at the Abbey, and afterwards Herbrand offered to send me to Whipsnade Zoo: 'There's nothing to do, you know.' I refused and walked to the Chinese Dairy alone.

Dinner a repetition of last night. Rough claret, and Herbrand puts a lot of ice in his. Miss Green's stinking dog sits on a tray on a high chair next to me. On the table is a wooden bowl hollowed out to hold a glass bowl full of ice. The dog licks the ice from time to time during dinner. Clear soup, choice of two fish, grouse, ice, peaches. AI.

I enclose a card stolen from my bedroom. 'You are particularly requested to refrain from giving a gratuity to any servant.'

It's been an experience coming here. Poor Herbrand! What an extraordinary business it is, and how odd that the world should contain places like Woburn and people like Herbrand. It sometimes strikes me as quite unnatural. My family is a zoo, only instead of lions and bears in cages there are unicorns, chimaeras, cockatrices and hippogriffs.

After the Duke's death in 1940 Conrad wrote to my mother:

If I had Woburn I'd make it a show place with restaurants, swimming pools, dance-halls, car parks, guides for four summer months and let the public have a good time . . .

A
Christmas
Cracker

1995

The Rev. Patrick Brontë is famous for having engendered his three still more famous daughters; few Brontë scholars, however, have remarked upon his own literary effusions, and in particular his invention of what must be the most irritating verse form ever devised. The idea of a serious limerick is somehow ridiculous enough – though I suppose such a thing might have been possible in the days before Edward Lear – but what about a limerick in which the last line makes no effort to rhyme with the first two? G. K. Chesterton, in his essay 'On Bad Poetry', quotes two examples, both from Brontë's 'The Village Maiden':

> To novels and plays not inclined,
> Nor aught that can sully her mind;
>   Temptations may shower,
>   Unmoved as a tower
> She quenches the fiery arrows.

and

> Religion makes beauty enchanting;
> And even where beauty is wanting,
>   The temper and mind
>   Religion-refined
> Will shine through the veil with sweet lustre.

The Dean of Divinity bets the Fellows' Chaplain in a bottle of Benedictine that it was Ignatius of Antioch, and not Polycarp of Smyrna, who yearned to be 'ground like wheat in the teeth of wild beasts'.

[*The Dean of Divinity won.*]

It was my son-in-law Antony Beevor who showed me this splendid passage in Reflections in a Silver Spoon *by Paul Mellon:*

. . . There was a forbidding quality in Father's cold attitude that always unnerved me and made it very difficult for me to pursue a personal conversation with him.

I sincerely believe, however, that the problem of communication rested with him as much as with me. To cite an example, he had written me a Christmas letter in 1929 from his Massachusetts Avenue apartment. It read:

Dear Paul,

As a birthday gift to you on reaching your majority last year I transferred to you 1000 shares preferred stock of the Aluminum Co. of America, as an outright gift.

Lately I transferred to you 2000 shares of the Monongahela St. Railway Co. This Monongahela St. Ry. stock is a gift to you which I make in consideration of your having given up or relinquished to your mother your interest or share in the Trust fund designated as Trust No. 3 of which the Union Trust Co. of Pittsburgh, Mr McCrory and I were Trustees. As you gave this to your mother at my instance I have made it up to you by gift of this stock.

With much love – Father

I think Father was trying in his own way in this letter to express his affection for me.

Joseph Paxton's account of his arrival at Chatsworth – as superintendent of gardens to the Duke of Devonshire – at the age of twenty-five:

I left London by the Comet Coach for Chesterfield; and arrived at Chatsworth at half-past four o'clock in the morning of the ninth of May, 1826. As no person was to be seen at that early hour, I got over the greenhouse gate by the old covered way, explored the pleasure grounds and looked round the outside of the house. I then went down to the kitchen gardens, scaled the outside wall and saw the whole of the place, set the men to work there at six o'clock; then returned to Chatsworth and got Thomas Weldon to play me the water works and afterwards went to breakfast with poor dear Mrs Gregory and her niece, the latter fell in love with me and I with her, and thus completed my first morning's work, at Chatsworth, before nine o'clock.

Perhaps the literary man
    I most admire among my betters
Is Richard Brinsley Sheridan
    Who, viewing life as more than letters,
Persisted, like a stubborn Gael,
    In not acknowledging his mail.

They say he hardly ever penned
    A proper 'Yrs. received and noted',
But spent what time he had to spend
    Shaping the law that England voted,
Or calling, on his comic flute,
    The tune for Captain Absolute.

Though chief of the prodigious wits,
    That Georgian taverns set to bubblin',
He did not answer 'Please Remits'
    Or scoldings from his aunts in Dublin.
Or birthday messages, or half
    The notes that begged an autograph.

I hear it sent his household wild –
    Became a sort of parlour fable –
The way that correspondence piled,
    Mountainous, upon his table,
While he ignored the double ring
    And wouldn't answer *anything*.

Not scrawls from friends nor screeds from foes
    Or scribble from the quibble-lover,
Or chits beginning 'I enclose
    Manuscript under separate cover,'
Or cards from people off on journeys,
    Or formal statements from attorneys.

The post came in. He let it lie.
   (All this biographers agree on.)
Especially he did not reply
   To things that had RSVP on.
Sometimes for months he dropped no lines
   To dear ones, or sent Valentines,

But, polishing a second act,
   Or coaxing Kings to license Freedom,
Let his epistles wait. In fact,
   They say he didn't even read 'em.
The which, some mornings, seems to me
   A glorious blow for Liberty.

Brave Celt! Although one must deplore
   His manners, and with reasons ample,
How bright, from duty's other shore,
   This moment seems his bold example!
And would I owned in equal balance
   His courage (and, of course, his talents).

Who, using up his mail to start
   An autumn fire or chink a crevice
Cried 'Letters longer are than art,
   But *vita* is extremely *brevis!*'
Then, choosing what was worth the candle,
   Sat down and wrote *The School for Scandal*.

                              Phyllis McGinley

As the time of rest, or of departure, approaches me, not only do many of the evils I had heard of, and prepared for, present themselves in more grievous shapes than I had expected; but one which I had scarcely ever heard of torments me increasingly every hour.

I had understood it to be in the order of things that the aged should lament their vanishing life as an instrument they had never used, now to be taken away from them; but not as an instrument, only then perfectly tempered and sharpened, and snatched out of their hands at the instant they could have done some real service with it. Whereas my own feeling, now, is that everything which has hitherto happened to me, or been done by me, whether well or ill, has been fitting me to take greater fortune more prudently, and do better work more thoroughly. And just when I seem to be coming out of school – very sorry to have been such a foolish boy, yet having taken a prize or two, and expecting to enter now upon some more serious business than cricket – I am dismissed by the Master I had hoped to serve, with a 'That's all I want of you, sir.'

So wrote John Ruskin in St Mark's Rest. *He may have been right in principle, but he was certainly wrong about himself. By 1877, when the book appeared, he was already fifty-eight and his insanity was beginning to take hold. All his best work had been done before he was fifty.*

Sybille Bedford said much the same thing as Ruskin, only in fewer words:

You see, when one's young one doesn't feel part of it yet, the human condition; one does things because they are not for good; everything is a rehearsal. To be repeated ad lib, to be put right when the curtain goes up in earnest. One day you know that the curtain was up all the time. That *was* the performance.

Mais elle était du monde, où les plus belles choses
Ont le pire destin;
Et rose, elle a vécu ce que vivent les roses,
L'espace d'un matin.

François de Malherbe (1555–1628) described these lovely lines as his 'consolation à Monsieur du Périer'. They bring us to the shortest sonnet ever written, given to me by my friend Robert Vaes. The author is unknown.

Fort
Belle
Elle
Dort.
Sort
Frêle
Quelle
Mort.
Rose
Close
La
Brise
L'a
Prise.

Mr Richard Tuely has kindly sent me a photocopy of this explanatory introduction to a booklet of post cards of Versailles, purchased by his mother in the 1920s:

Raise up by Louis XIV on the village's employment of this name, Versailles was at the origine a little castle serving for a meetting of chasing.

From his majorite Louis XIV particulary affectionate it doing fence, which the Palace is the central Court of Marble.

Mansard been the genius architecte of this illustre Versailles of the only Residence of the world wich the construction's valour is about 500 millions. Le Notre, the creator of those garden, of this beautiful park, of those wall's foliage, of those infinite alley overshadow.

Peopled by marble's world wich the Goddess and the heros seems to raise the guard onder the Roi Soleil's abode.

Fascinate gardens wich sparkling sheaf shooting, the complicated and multiple shoots, sumptuous frame of wonderful feast wich Louis XIV offer very often to the court. Silent grove, agreeable green grass. Complete successfully the Palace, evering things are harmony and nobleness.

The interior of the palace subimt with every Kingdom lots modification. The apartments of Louis XV, the fine wainscot skulte are wonderful, light and delightfull decoration, it is all the art of the XVIII cent.

The little apartments regulate to Marie-Antoinette are chefs d'oeuvre of the pure and dainty style from that epoch.

The palace of Versailles been invade by the people on the nights of 5th and 6th October 1789 and Marie Antoinette's guards saved her with favour and devotdness. It is only on Louis Philippe that the palace received the actual distination, the furnished apartments ussing have been spread about by the revolution, the great apartments been transform of History Museum The Great Trianon was the residence of Louis XIV and Napoleon.

The furniture been renew by Napoleon. The Little Trianon raise up by Gabriel and offer by Louis XVI to Marie Antoinette was the place of predilection of this queen wich it been enclose by charming park where exalt the Pavillon's music and the Temple of Love elegance and gracefull edifice.

To take one pleasure of diversion she amused her self at the farmer wife a miniature hamlet been raise up withe grac and affected wich the disturbance revolutionist surprised her and swept her for ever.

The difference between you and her
(Whom I to you did once prefer)
Is clear enough to settle:
She like a diamond shone, but you
Shine like an early drop of dew
Poised on a red rose-petal.

The dewdrop carries in its eye
Mountain and forest, sea and sky,
With every change of weather;
Contrariwise, the diamond splits
The prospect into idle bits
That none can piece together.

                              Robert Graves

I disapprove in general of lifting from other people's anthologies; but when I came across the following review from a Nevada newspaper (of 23 March 1983) in Words about Music, *by John Amis and Michael Rose, an exception had to be made:*

ZUCKERMAN DAZZLES LAS VEGANS

Wednesday January 18, Pinchas Zuckerman conducted and performed with the St Paul Chamber Orchestra in an all Betthoven [*sic*] concert at Ham Hall. Those Las Vegans lucky enough to attend were treated to an evening of performance of a calibre shamefully rare in a city of half a million people.

The first half of the program, consisting of the Overture to the Creatures of Prometheus and the Symphony No. 4 in B flat, Op. 60, was somewhat disappointing in that Zuckerman conducted the orchestra with his back to the audience. While one cannot fault him entirely for assuming the traditional posture of the vast majority of great maestros, it must be said that the choice of his stance in combination with his having also elected to wear the traditional 'tails' all but obscured whatever clarity of physique one might have hoped to savor, even from the best seats.

Even so, true genius shines forth. The broad expanse of his shoulders, the abundant wavy dark hair, the well proportioned legs planted oh-so-firmly on the podium were sufficient food for the culture-starved crowd to feast upon throughout even the longest of movements. Perhaps it might even be said that the program order reflected a certain deftness of planning, for it certainly left the audience at intermission clambering to return to their seats in anticipation of the climactic second half which promised the chance to observe Mr Zuckerman from the front for the duration of the whole violin concerto.

What followed was pure magic, as Zuckerman proved that the combination of virtuosity, artistry and a great body can make even the Concerto in D for Violin and Orchestra, Op. 61, seem too short. He inspired his audience where a performer of lesser attributes might have left them bored to death. But who among them could for an instant let her eyes stray from the Maestro as he cradled his violin so gently, yet firmly, with the touch of well proportioned hands made strong and supple by years of torturous practice? Whose eyes could have been other than riveted to the spectacle of the grace and power of the bow arm, the fire in his dark eyes, the tension in his taut thighs as he made ready to launch into some passionate passage with the energy of an athlete? Who could but succumb to the tenderness of his smile as he lost himself in the ecstacy [*sic*] of each undulating sweet melodic phrase that surged and swelled from the instrument at his command? It is only a wonder that the audience managed to suppress both thunderous applause and shrieks of pleasure until the end. We can only hope that it not be an eternity before he again graces our stage with the captivating magic of his talents.

Mr Zuckerman is a native of Israel, Middle East. He has recorded quite a number of musical pieces on to records which are considered quite good by those who listen to them. He is married to a woman of questionable musical ability and character.

Lisa Coffey

And here is another piece of music criticism, rather shorter but perhaps rather more perceptive, by the American composer Virgil Thompson on the playing of Dame Myra Hess:

Not memorable like a love affair, but satisfactory like a good tailor.

Many years ago – it was actually in the 1978 Cracker – I quoted Keats's marvellous lines:

> . . . as when heaved anew,
> Old ocean rolls a lengthened wave to shore
> Down whose green back the short-lived foam, all hoar,
> Bursts gradual, with a wayward indolence

together with a passage from the short story 'In Dreams begin Responsibilities' by Delmore Schwartz:

The ocean is becoming rough; the waves come in slowly, tugging strength from far back. The moment before they somersault, the moment when they arch their backs so beautifully, showing green and white veins amid the black, that moment is intolerable. They finally crack, dashing fiercely upon the sand, actually driving, full force downward against the sand, bouncing upward and forward, and at last petering out into a small stream which races up the beach and then is recalled.

Here are two more on the same theme. First, Tennyson:

> The great waters break,
> Whitening for half a league and thin themselves,
> Far over sands marbled with moon and cloud.

> *Idylls of the King: The Last Tournament*

And Shakespeare, from Timon of Athens:

> Lie where the light foam of the sea may beat
> Thy grave-stone daily.

From the diary of Virginia Woolf, 31 August 1928:

This is the last day of August and like almost all of them of extraordinary beauty. Each day is fine enough and hot enough for sitting out; but also full of wandering clouds; and that fading and rising of the light which so enraptures me in the Downs; which I am always comparing to the light beneath an alabaster bowl. The corn is now stood about in rows of three, four or five solid shaped yellow cakes – rich, it seems, with eggs and spice; good to eat. Sometimes I see the cattle galloping 'like mad' as Dostoievsky would say, in the brooks. The clouds – if I could describe them I would; one yesterday had flowing hair on it, like the very fine white hair of an old man. At this moment they are white in a leaden sky; but the sun behind the house is making the grass green. I walked to the racecourse today and saw a weasel.

We trained hard; but it seemed that every time we were beginning to form into teams we would be reorganized. I was to learn later in life that we tend to meet any new situation by reorganizing; and a wonderful method it can be for creating the illusion of progress while producing confusion, inefficiency and demoralization.

Gaius Petronius (Arbiter)
Trimalchio's Feast

[This was given me years ago by my old friend John Grey (Jock) Murray; I'm sure he never doubted its authenticity. Recently, however, during a Quote – Unquote *radio programme in which I took part, Nigel Rees maintained that nobody had been able to find it anywhere in Petronius. You have been warned.]*

On a rusty iron throne
Past the furthest star of space,
I saw Satan sit alone.
Old and haggard was his face;
For his work was done, and he
Rested in eternity.

And to him from out the sun
Came his father and his friend,
Saying, 'Now the work is done,
Enmity is at an end.'
And he guided Satan to
Paradises that he knew.

Gabriel without a frown,
Uriel without a spear,
Raphael came singing down,
Welcoming their ancient peer;
And they seated him beside
One who had been crucified.

James Stephens

*Verbs are always the most difficult part of any language, but does one have to
make quite such heavy weather of them as does J. W. Redhouse in his* Ottoman
Turkish Grammar? *It was published in 1884 and brought to my notice by John
Parker. In full, this conjugation continues for thirteen pages; but the following
extracts should be enough to give the flavour:*

THE FIRST COMPLEX CATEGORY

Infinitive:	*teper olmaq*	To be a willing, natural, determined, constant or habitual kicker; to be kicking; to kick (habitually).
Imperative:	*teper ol*	Be thou kicking; kick thou (habitually).
Past:	*teper olur idim*	I used to be always kicking; I would be, or would have been, always kicking.
Future:	*teper olajaghdim*	I am about to become a constant kicker.

Necessitative

Past:	*teper olmaliyidim*	I ought to have been a constant kicker.

Optative

Aorist:	*teper olayim*	That I may be a constant kicker.

Passive participles

Future:	*teper olajaq*	Whom, which (I, etc.) am about constantly to kick.

Verbal nouns

Future:	*teper olajaq*	The act of being about (now) to become (hereafter) a constant kicker.

THE SECOND COMPLEX CATEGORY

Future:	*tepmish olajaghim*	I am about becoming one who has kicked; I am going to have kicked.

Necessitative

Past:	*tepmish olmaliyidim*	I must (then) have (already) kicked (before).

Verbal Nouns

Present:	*tepmish olma*	The (present state of) having (already) kicked.

Gerunds

2nd:	*tepmish olaraq*	Having the continued quality of having kicked (and . . .)
3rd:	*tepmish olunja*	As soon as (is, was, will be) one who *or* which has kicked . . .

THE THIRD COMPLEX CATEGORY

Present:	*tepejek oliyorim*	I am (often) on the point of kicking; I become on the point . . .

Active Participles

Aorist:	*tepejek olur*	Who *or* which is (naturally) *or* will be (some time) on the point of kicking.
Future:	*tepejek olajaq*	*Not used, as being cacophonous.*

When thou must home to shades of underground,
And there arriv'd, a new admired guest,
The beauteous spirits do ingirt thee round,
White Iope, blithe Helen, and the rest,
To hear the stories of thy finisht love
From that smoothe tongue whose musicke hell can move;

Then wilt thou speake of banqueting delights,
Of masks and revels which sweete youth did make,
Of Turnies and great challenges of knights,
And all these triumphs for thy beauties sake:
When thou hast told these honours done to thee,
Then tell, O tell, how thou didst murther me.

Thomas Campion
(1567–1620)

On 18 March 1646, the Commonwealth army of Sir Thomas Fairfax was drawn up below Pendennis Castle in Cornwall, which was held by the seventy-year-old Sir John Arundell. Fairfax sent up a message, calling on the garrison to surrender and demanding a reply within two hours. He got one, a good deal more quickly than he expected. It read as follows:

Sir,

The Castle was committed to my Government by his Majesty, who by our laws hath Command of the castles and Forts of this Kingdom; and my age of seventy summons me hence shortly. Yet I shall desire no other testimony to follow my departure than my conscience to God and loyalty to his Majesty, whereto I am bound by all the obligations of nature, duty and oath. I wonder you demand the Castle without authority from his Majesty, which if I should render, I brand myself and my posterity with the indelible charge of Treason. And having taken less than two minutes' resolution, I resolve that I will here bury myself before I deliver up this Castle to such as fight against his Majesty, and that nothing you can threaten is formidable to me in respect of the loss of loyalty and conscience.

Your servant

John Arundell, of Trerice

He held out for five months before surrendering on honourable terms.

Random reflections on life:

> The rain it raineth every day
> Upon the just and unjust fella,
> But chiefly on the just, because
> The unjust steals the just's umbrella.

[This sad reflection proves to be by Lord Bowen (1835–94), a much-loved judge who, according to the Dictionary of National Biography, *was in his youth said by his brother to be 'the only man I ever knew who could jump a cow as it stood'.]*

> Shake and shake the ketchup bottle;
> None'll come and then a lot'll.

> For Thy coming, Lord, we pray,
> But let it be some other day;
> On Thy return our hopes are set –
> Thy will be done, but not just yet.

and, from my old and sadly missed friend William Hayter:

> Heaven above
> And hell below;
> The one we love;
> The other, no.

In The Italians, *Luigi Barzini attributes to 'the husband of an eighteenth-century ballerina' the reflection:*

> Les cornes, c'est comme les dents. Ça fait mal quand ça pousse, et puis l'on mange avec.

And finally, a favourite saying of another old chum, Bernard Levin:

> Alkohol und Nikotin
> Rafft die halbe Menschheit hin;
> Ohne Alkohol und Rauch
> Stirbt die andere Hälfte auch.

which might be not very elegantly translated:

> Alcohol and nicotine
> Snatch half the people from the scene;
> Deprived of alcohol and smokes
> There follow all the other blokes.

Possible contenders for the Oddest Title of the Year Competition, 1994, run by the Diagram Group:

Septic Tanks and Cesspools: A Do-It-Yourself Guide, written and published by Peter Jobling.

Butchering Livestock at Home, by Phyllis Hobson (Garden Way Publishing).

Japanese Chins, by Claude Alexander (THF Publications).

Illustrated Encyclopedia of Metal Lunch Boxes, by Allan Woodall (Schiffer Publications).

101 Super Uses for Tampon Applicators, by Lori Katz and Barbara Mayer (PBS).

Psychiatric Disorders in Dental Practice, by M. D. Enoch and R. G. Jagger (John Wright).

Gymnastics for Horses, by Eleanor Russell (Teal Publishing).

Best Bike Rides in the Mid-Atlantic, by Trudy F. Bell (Globe Pequot Press).

Scenes of Seduction: Prostitution, Hysteria and Reading Differences in Nineteenth Century France, by Jane Matlock (Columbia University Press).

In the churchyard of Nevern, Dyfed, is a gravestone bearing the following inscription:

To the memory of ANNALITITIA and GEORGE, children of the Revd. DAVID GRIFFITH, VICAR of this Parish, who died in their Infancy, AD 1794.

> They tasted of life's bitter cup,
> Refused to drink the potion up;
> But turned their little heads aside
> Disgusted with the taste – and died.

On the tomb of a rich mill-owner of Corsham, Wiltshire:

> The labouring poor he never did condemn,
> And God enriched him by the means of them.

And in the church of Maids' Moreton, Buckinghamshire, a wall tablet to the memory of Penelope Verney, wife of Lord Willoughby de Broke, reads:

> Underneath this stone doth lye
> As much virtue as could dye
> Which when alive did vigour give
> To as much beauty as could live.

Sir Winston Churchill on General Sir Redvers Buller (1839–1908):

Certainly he was a man of a considerable scale. He plodded on from blunder to blunder and from one disaster to another, without losing either the regard of his country or the trust of his troops, to whose feeding as well as to his own he paid serious attention.

My friend Dr Lionel Dakers, former Director of the Royal School of Church Music, has introduced me to the writings of the Rev. J. M. C. Crum, for many years a canon of Canterbury. Canon Crum wrote a number of remarkable hymns, of which the following – included in the original edition of The Church and School Hymnal *– provides an example:*

> O once in a while we obey with a smile
>   And are ever so modest and prudent;
> But it's not very long before something is wrong,
>   And somebody's done what he shouldn't.
>
> In meadow and wood the cattle are good,
>   And the rabbits are thinking no evil,
> The anemones white are refined and polite,
>   And all the primroses are civil.
>
> O Saviour, look down when we sulk or we frown,
>   And smooth into kindness our quarrels;
> Till our heart is as light as a little bird's flight
>   And our life is as free as a squirrel's.

The canon's published works include, I understand, 'Road Mending on the Sacred Way' (1924) and 'What Mean Ye by these Stones?' (1926).

[Few items in any Cracker have ever brought me as many letters as this one – several from people who actually knew Canon Crum. The late Sir David Hunt, who once heard him preach, wrote:

Memories of his sermon were long treasured by his hearers. It was more absurdly risible than the hymn you quote, but the delivery was what increased the amusement. If you remember the actor Robertson Hare you will have a good idea. The text and the message elude my memory: all that remains is his wide-eyed and enthusiastic quotation:

> 'Oh blackbird, what a boy you are!
> How you do go it!'

Michael Gill writes:

Growing up as a boy in Canterbury in the 1930s, it was impossible not to know Canon Crum. Quite apart from the violet and purple magnificence of Cosmo Lang – more like a Renaissance cardinal than an Anglican archbishop – the authority of the living cathedral was made manifest to the town by two opposing figures: the tall-striding, tightly gaitered and imperiously profiled Red Dean, Hewlett Johnson; and the fluttering, wavering, indecisive progress of the saintly canon, sicklied o'er with the pale cast of thought and incapable of the half dozen steps needed to cross the busy Mercery Lane.

Canon Crum, as I remember, lived in one of the Tudor houses that decorated the south-east end of the cathedral close. All these lovely old places were burnt down in the terrible fire raid of June 1 1942. The canon survived and moved into a hotel on the High Street. There, some five months later, he was having his weekly bath. (The use of water was strictly limited in wartime; even the King had to be satisfied with three inches in the tub.) Suddenly, without any warning, the low-level daylight raid of October 31 began. The first sticks of bombs fell deafeningly close. The canon leaped out of his bath and ran into the corridor, bumping into a maid running in the opposite direction. Propriety won the day. The canon rushed back to the shelter of the bath. The next stick of bombs scored a direct hit. The front wall of the hotel collapsed and the canon, unhurt but still unclothed, slid in his bath down the rubble into the High Street.

Peggie Richardson, who knew him well when her father was Dean, loved him:

He was wonderfully unworldly, very wise, very charming, and above everything else he was a scholar. His sermons were a delight, erudite and poetical. He said to us once 'I sit here in my study and read and read and read, and no one is any the wiser.']

[And then, I must shamefully confess, I repeated myself yet again, ending the Cracker with the same little poem that I had used in 1991. What can I have been thinking of? But the mistake led to a surprising discovery, revealed to me by Linda Kelly: that this wry little verse wasn't by Victor Hugo as I had always believed (or by Alfred de Musset as Evelyn Waugh had always believed) but by a little-known poet called Léon Montenaeken, of whom I had never heard. It comes, I gather from a volume called Peu de Chose *– which, of course, it is.]*

> La vie est vaine,
> Un peu d'amour,
> Un peu de peine,
> Et puis, bonjour!
>
> La vie est brève,
> Un peu d'espoir,
> Un peu de rêve,
> Et puis, bonsoir!

Bonus

The following poem was written by William Pakenham Walsh – later Bishop of Ossory, Ferns and Leighlin – in 1832, when he was twelve:

A DIRTY NIGHT ON THE FASTNET ROCK

Oh flutes! The night came on.
The grizzly, guzzling, gulping night,
And oh Great Scott what mud, what rain, what scrunch!
The rain came down in streams –
'Twas not the spitting, cat-like rain, oh no! –
It was the swilling, swelching, Swithian rain
That makes the new rags and the old alike smell wet,
The sousing, duck-loved rain.

The wind grew worse; oh slithering snow shoes how it squelched!
It screeched around the lighthouse like some green-eyed fiend –
Great Scotland Yard what shrieks!
The one-stringed fiddle or the untuned flute were music to those
    shrieks;
The swinging, swelching, slobbering waves came lamming on the rocks,
The gulching, sea-green waves.
And as I looked I saw an awful distant sky-high wave,
Land's End it was a wave!
Afar it seemed an oily, bloated, bulging wave, but near
It was a swearing, oathing, spiteful wave!
Buzzing along
A Boss-Eyed Shaker . . . a beastly wave.

Great Scott! It nears the rock,
The many-cornered, wave-dividing rock.
It humped itself upon its strong hind legs, and then it burst,
It more than burst, it bust, it simply bashed,
It lit upon the blistered rock and swept away the lighthouse lamp,
The beastly oily lighthouse lamp.

Oh Hares! Oh Jumping Crimes!
Oh shattering chandeliers and fizzing squish!
Oh creeping crocodiles and crippled crabs!

It gulched and slooched around the scraggy lighthouse rock,
The well-pecked lobster rock.

Oh flutes! The night came on –
The grizzly, grimy, black-eyed night, a night
That gloried in being black.
My tooth-gnawed pen can ill describe the inky darkness
Of that congealed black.
Suffice to say the unwashed negro or the Patagonian slug
Would shine like muzzled virtue next that black.

But hold! What is that shadowy form?
    Oh scootling wizards! Can I see aright?
A ship! An uncouth, ghastly, scarecrow ship!
    With fear I shrink away, and like the unspun spinning top . . .
    I hold my breath.

Oh snakes! She nears the rock.
The many-cornered, wave-dividing rock –
Oh splathering toads! I see the masts and gear,
The spinning wheel, the death's head on the prow.
I see the horror-stricken victims clinging to the ropes,
A ghastly lot, unshaven, a filthy, dirty, beastly-looking crew
Huddled upon an unscrubbed, an unswabbed and unsqueegeed deck –
    Oh one-eyed Crusoe let me die unknown,
    A gasping codfish on some puffin's isle,
But never let me gaze again on such a sight!

On came the humping bulging waves
Bearing their wobbling craft,
The hog-backed, quivering, floundering craft.
Oh staggering jelly how she reels,
Oh shivering custard and oh writhing eels,
Oh bandaged thunder and oh lightning greased,
    Oh palsied, lurching, epileptic funk,
    With one last agonizing buck-jump leap
She's whizzed a splathered wreck upon the rock . . .
    And sunk!

A
Christmas
Cracker

1996

From With the Flag on the Seven Seas: Fifty Years a Seafarer *by the splendidly named Admiral Sir Bulwark Bloode, published in 1907:*

The Pacific Station had its ups and downs. My first mission when I took command of the *Myrmidon* was to track down some Solomon Islanders who had eaten a Quaker missionary. By all accounts he was a strange fellow who did not drink nor eat meat and walked around barefoot. It seems he stuck his nose into some native war and got eaten for his troubles. The poor devil was wrapped in palm leaves, parboiled in salt water and then lightly grilled.

[But see now p. 258.]

PRINTER'S ERROR

As o'er my latest book I pored,
　　Enjoying it immensely,
I suddenly exclaimed 'Good Lord!'
　　And gripped the volume tensely.
'Golly!' I cried, I writhed in pain,
'They've done it on me once again!'
　　And furrows creased my brow.
I'd written (which I thought quite good)
'Ruth, ripening into womanhood,
Was now a girl who knocked men flat
And frequently got whistled at';
And some vile, careless, casual gook
Had spoiled the best thing in the book
　　By printing 'not'
　　(Yes, 'not', great Scott!)
　　When I had written 'now'.

On murder in the first degree
　　The Law, I know, is rigid:
Its attitude, if A kills B,
　　To A is always frigid.
It counts it not a trivial slip
If, on behalf of authorship,
You liquidate compositors.
This kind of conduct it abhors
　　And seldom will allow.
Nevertheless, I deemed it best
And in the public interest
To buy a gun, to oil it well,
Inserting what is called a shell,
And go and pot with sudden shot
This printer who had printed 'not'
　　When I had written 'now'.

I tracked the bounder to his den
　　Through private information:
I said 'Good afternoon' and then
　　Explained the situation:
'I'm not a fussy man,' I said,

'I smile when you put "rid" for "red"
And "bad" for "bed" and "hoad" for "head"
   And "bolge" instead of "bough".
When "wone" appears in lieu of "wine"
Or if you alter "Cohn" to "Schine"
   I never make a row.
I know how easy errors are;
But this time you have gone too far
By printing "not" when you knew what
I really wrote was "now".
Prepare,' I said, 'to meet your God
Or, as you'd say, your Goo or Bod
   Or possibly your Gow.'

A few weeks later into court
   I came to stand my trial.
The judge was quite a decent sort,
   He said 'Well, cocky, I'll
Be passing sentence in a jiff,
And so, my poor unhappy stiff,
If you have anything to say,
Now is the moment. Fire away.
   You have?' I said: 'And how!
Me lud, the facts I don't dispute:
I did, I own it freely, shoot
This printer through the collar stud.
What else could I have, done, me lud?
      He'd printed "not"' –
      The judge said: 'What?
   When you had written "now"?
God bless my soul! Gadzooks!' said he,
'The blighters did that once to me.
   A dirty trick, I trow.
I hereby quash and override
The jury's verdict. Gosh!' he cried,
'Give me your hand. Yes, I insist,
You splendid fellow! Case dismissed.'
   (Cheers, and a voice 'Wow-wow!')

A statue stands against the sky,
   Lifelike, and rather pretty;
'Twas recently erected by
   The P.E.N. Committee.

And many a passer-by is stirred
For on the plinth, if that's the word,
In golden letters you may read:
'This is the man who did the deed.
    His hand set to the plough,
He did not sheathe his sword, but got
A gun at great expense, and shot
The human blot who'd printed "not"
    When he had written "now".
He acted with no thought of self,
Not for advancement, not for pelf,
But just because it made him hot
To think the man had printed "not"
When he had written "now".'

[*Cotton Mather, a peculiarly unpleasant Presbyterian divine of Boston, Mass., wrote in his book* Magnalia Christi Americana *(which is also a commentary on the Salem witchcraft trials of 1692):*

Reader, *Carthagenia* was of the mind, that unto those *Three Things* which the Ancients held Impossible, there should be added this *fourth*, to find a Book printed without *Errata's*. It seems, the Hands of *Briareus*, and the Eyes of *Argus*, will not prevent them.]

While we are on the subject, I remember that most distinguished man of the law Sydney Kentridge, Q. C. telling me some years ago that wherever there is a difference between author and publisher we have only to turn to the summing-up of Lord Abinger, C. B., in the case of Fraser v. Berkeley *(Court of Exchequer, 1836), when the Hon. Grantley Berkeley had assaulted Mr Fraser for publishing an attack on him and his family in the guise of a review of his novel,* Berkeley Castle. *The judge concluded:*

> I really think that this assault was carried to a very inconsiderate length, and that if an author is to go and give a beating to a publisher who has offended him, two or three blows with a horsewhip ought to be quite enough to satisfy his irritated feelings.

You cannot bring about prosperity by discouraging thrift. You cannot strengthen the weak by weakening the strong. You cannot help the wage earner by pulling down the wage payer. You cannot further the brotherhood of man by encouraging class hatred. You cannot help the poor by destroying the rich. You cannot keep out of trouble by spending more than you earn. You cannot build character and courage by taking away man's initiative and independence. You cannot help men permanently by doing for them what they could and should do for themselves.

[I attributed these words to Abraham Lincoln, as had Republican Congresswoman Frances P. Bolton of Ohio, who read them into the Congressional Record on 25 January 1949. It turns out, however, that we were both wrong. They were actually written by a Presbyterian clergyman, the Rev. William J. H. Boetcker. But they seem to me none the worse for that.]

Since 1996 marks the centenary of the publication of A. E. Housman's A Shropshire Lad, this affectionate little verse by my friend Roy Dean, crossword-solver and palindromist extraordinaire, may not come amiss:

A SHROPSHIRE LASS

In spring the hawthorn scatters
Its snow along the hedge,
And thoughts of country matters
Run strong on Wenlock Edge.

So fared I, loose and feckless,
And met a maiden fair;
She wore an amber necklace
To match her tawny hair.

Her mouth was soft and willing,
Her eyes were like the sea;
I offered her a shilling
If she would lie with me.

At that she blushed so sweetly,
And cast her fine eyes down;
Then, whispering discreetly,
Suggested half a crown.

Two letters from the Duke of Wellington: the first to the Foreign Office, 1812:

Gentlemen,

Whilst marching to Portugal to a position which commands the approach to Madrid and the French forces, my officers have been diligently complying with your requests, which have been sent by HM ship from London to Lisbon and then by dispatch rider to our headquarters.

We have enumerated our saddles, bridles, tents and tent poles, and all manner of sundry items for which His Majesty's Government holds me accountable. I have dispatched reports on the character, wit and spleen of every officer. Each item and every farthing has been accounted for, with two regrettable exceptions for which I beg your indulgence.

Unfortunately the sum of one shilling and ninepence remains unaccounted for in one infantry battalion's petty cash, and there has been a hideous confusion as to the number of jars of raspberry jam issued to one cavalry regiment during a sandstorm in western Spain. This reprehensive carelessness may be related to the pressure of circumstance, since we are at war with France, a fact which may come as a bit of a surprise to you gentlemen in Whitehall.

This brings me to my present purpose, which is to request elucidation of my instructions from His Majesty's Government, so that I may better understand why I am dragging an army over these barren plains. I construe that perforce it must be one of two alternative duties, as given below. I shall pursue either one with the best of my ability, but I cannot do both:

1. To train an army of uniformed British clerks in Spain for the benefit of the accountant and copy boys in London; or, perchance,

2. To see to it that the forces of Napoleon are driven out of Spain.

I have the honour, etc.

Wellington

The second, to the Reverend William Coldwell, Rector of Stafford:

The Duke of Wellington presents his compliments to Mr Coldwell. As Mr Coldwell feels that his application to the Duke needs apology, the Duke will say nothing further on the subject. But he must say that as there is not a church, chapel, school or glebe house, or even pagoda, built in any part from the North to the South Pole, or the utmost limits of the Earth, to which he is not called upon to contribute, it is not surprising that Mr Coldwell, having got £7,500 for the restoration of his church, should call upon the Duke to contribute, who has nothing to say to Stafford or to Staffordshire.

[The first of these letters has aroused scepticism among a number of my friends. Was raspberry jam really issued to the army during the Peninsular War? And did it (the army, not the raspberry jam) include dispatch riders?

On consideration, I confess to feeling a bit doubtful myself – especially since I stupidly made no note of where I found this item. I am reluctant to believe that it is a complete fabrication, if only because I can't see why anyone should have bothered to make it up. Could it, I wonder, be based on a genuine letter, whose text has got somehow corrupted?]

My daughter Artemis came across the following story while researching her book Cairo in the War. *In the year 641* AD, *during the first irrepressible surge of the Muslim conquests, Egypt fell to the Arab general Amr. Of him E. M. Forster writes – in his* History and Guide to Alexandria – *that 'he was not only a great general, he was an administrator, a delightful companion, and a poet – one of the ablest and most charming men that Islam ever produced.' A few years later, Forster tells us, he died at Fostat, a city that he himself founded and that was the germ of modern Cairo.*

As he lay on his couch a friend said to him: 'You have often remarked that you would like to find an intelligent man at the point of death, and ask him what his feelings were. Now I ask *you* that question.' Amr replied: 'I feel as if the heaven lay close upon the earth and I between the two, breathing through the eye of a needle.'

They climbed on sketchy ladders towards God,
With winch and pulley hoisted hewn rock into heaven,
Inhabited sky with hammers, defied gravity,
Deified stone, took up God's house to meet Him.

And came down to their suppers and small beer;
Every night slept, lay with their smelly wives,
Quarrelled and cuffed the children, lied,
Spat, sang, were happy or unhappy.

And every day took to the ladders again;
Impeded the rights of way of another summer's
Swallows, grew greyer, shakier, became less inclined
To fix a neighbour's roof of a fine evening.

Saw naves sprout arches, clerestories soar,
Cursed the loud fancy glaziers for their luck,
Somehow escaped the plague, got rheumatism,
Decided it was time to give it up,

To leave the spire to others; stood in the crowd
Well back from the vestments at the consecration,
Envied the fat bishop his warm boots,
Cocked up a squint eye and said, 'I bloody did that.'

John Ormond

Or, as T. E. Hulme once reminded us:

Old houses were scaffolding once,
And workmen whistling.

One of the great treats of the 1960s was the weekly reading, in the Observer and the Sunday Times, of the property advertisements of Roy Brooks. Mr Brooks was an estate agent – but an estate agent with a difference, as a few of his notices make abundantly clear:

WANTED: Someone with taste, means and a stomach strong enough to buy this erstwhile house of ill repute in Pimlico. It is untouched by the 20th century as far as convenience or even the basic human decencies are concerned. Although it reeks of damp or worse, the plaster is coming off the walls and daylight peeps through a hole in the roof, it is still habitable judging by the bed of rags, fag ends and empty bottles in one corner. Plenty of scope for the socially aspiring to express their decorative taste and get their abode in the glossies, and nothing to stop them putting Westminster on their notepaper. 10 rather unpleasant rooms with slimy back yard. £4,650 Freehold. Tarted up, these houses make £15,000.

WESTMORELAND Terrace, Westminster, SW1: Mod. Luxury Architect Res., one of four built where three stood before, so don't expect big rms; but ideal for, say, Japanese family. Owner, from N. Australia has no objection to Japs – in Pimlico. VIEW OF RIVER from 2 rms – just. GARAGE. A GIFT AT £10,550 FHLD.; TRY ANY OFFER.

£4,250 TRY ANY OFFER. Forced to move nearer his lab, and hush-hush work on electronic mousetrap (still on the secret list), B.Sc. of safely negative political opinions sacrifices comfortable and stately mock Tudor (1936) res. halfway between Bushey and Richmond Parks (abt. 20 mins. Waterloo). Dble. drawing rm leads to dining section making a surprisingly fine 30ft rm (FINE PARQUET FLOOR) leading to rose gdn and sacred gooseberry bush. (Strange myths still linger in the suburbs . . .)

BARNES COMMON: With 2 stations, Green Line and other buses escape is easy from this quiet, respectable suburb. A well-built EDWARDIAN FAMILY RES, 24ft. dble. drawing rm, 4 bedrms, 3 good but cheese-shaped, the 4th would only comfortably accommodate a triangular door. In the doctor's bedrm, hundreds of books COMPLETELY lined the walls, revealing only the mauve ceiling. Garage and garden with what the Dr. describes as 'the rather attractive back passage'. Terrific bargain only £6,625 FREEHOLD.

FASHIONABLE Blackheath Park . . . Anthropologist, having completed his studies on the Space Man and going to Scotland to study Pictish burials, leaves his OPUNTIA GIGANTICARIX. (You wouldn't get this monster housebound 7ft. cactus out without a fight anyway.) BARGAIN £7,990.

£3,500 FREEHOLD. The airy, elegant SPAN HOUSE of England's Design Consultant of sanitary ware, lampposts and other modern conveniences: forced out by fecundity. Owner eschewing Sabbatical pistol practice will show today.

ONE OF THE BIG POTS in Chamber Music, leader of a famous quartet, taking up suburban residence with former girl viola pupil, SACRIFICES exciting, newly-built ('55) w2 MEWS RES. . . 'Library' with bookshelves, all of 8ft sq. – suit erudite dwarf.

Sir Edward Burne-Jones writes to William Allingham:

My dear,

Come and stay with us: I want to see you and jaw about things –
the garden is full pleasant.

Gabriel [D. G. Rossetti] has a wombat. He has written about it to
this effect:

> Oh how the family affections combat
> Within my breast! Each hour throws a bomb at
> My burning soul – neither from owl or from bat
> Can peace be gained, until I clasp my wombat . . .

*[The year was 1857. Readers wishing to research the subject further are referred to
Michael Archer's article 'Rossetti and the Wombat' in* Apollo, *March 1965.]*

March 1995

Dearest Tamara,

You ask me how I remember Wogan's paintings. First I recall the well-being with which he painted. Legs apart, feet firmly on the ground, and the brushes in his hand like the rod of a water-diviner. In painting, he searched for the good, the good and the simple. And the paintings he left behind are there to remind us. He left them, like he would leave a jug of milk on the kitchen table of the farm in the Cotswolds, or a dressing-gown on the hook of the door of a bedroom where a guest slept, or a pair of binoculars on a windowsill looking out on to the hills. His paintings too are an expression of hospitality. He painted like a host who wanted everyone to be happy in his house, and for that happiness he fought all his life against the odds.

One could see it in his face. He had the face of somebody who has survived the long night and is determined to live the next day well with his friends. As a man he was a stoic, as a painter he became a child. The painting took the hand of the man and walked beside him towards what both thought was the promised city. A little like the one Lorenzetti painted in the Allegory of Good Government.

He had no claims for his own painting and was excessively modest. But in the act of painting he believed fervently. I think he would have said, like Shitao the eighteenth-century Chinese master of landscape: 'The brush is there to bring things back from chaos.' And this too is a form of hospitality.

Wogan would have liked, I think, another quotation from Shitao and would have smiled, happy, at the idea of putting it here: 'The first brush stroke included everything that existed in the universe; the painting receives from the ink, the ink receives from the brush, the brush receives from the hand, the hand receives from the heart; all this is like the sky conceiving what the earth finishes, for everything is the fruit of receiving.'

I see his eyes creased in pleasure . . .

With my love,

John

OLD-FASHIONED Vicar (Tractarian) seeks colleague. Left-hand fast bowler preferred. Good golf handicap an asset but not essential. Fine church with good musical tradition. Parish residential and farming. Box HV 521.

The Church Times,
30 June 1967

For many years I assumed that this particular form of muscular Christianity had had its day. Then, on 25 June 1992, the following letter appeared in the correspondence columns of The Times; *and I wasn't so sure.*

Sir,

Last Sunday I dragged myself away from watching the end of the Test match at Lord's in order to preach at our evening service on the theme of 'What Christians believe about the Trinity'. The last three balls I watched being bowled were by Ian Salisbury, England's exciting new spin bowler. The first was a leg-spinner, the second a top-spinner, the third a googly.

I had been ferreting around for a helpful illustration of the Trinity – and there it was: one person expressing himself in three different, but very similar ways. The leg-spinner's stock ball represents God the Father, who created us to 'feel after him'; the top-spinner, which goes straight through, represents the direct activity of God the Son; the googly represents the surprising activity of God the Holy Spirit.

Yours sincerely

David Prior

St Michael's Church
4 Chester Square
London SW1

[Pat Gibson tells me how Joyce Grenfell used to recall with delight overhearing one of a group of army padres, on their way to join the troops in the Middle East, say to a friend on the dockside: 'I say, old chap, have you seen my communion tackle? I can't find it anywhere.']

Two views on poetry. First, that of Byron, writing to Thomas Moore:

I can never get people to understand that poetry is the expression of *excited passion*, and that there is no such thing as a life of passion any more than a continuous earthquake or an eternal fever. Besides, who would ever *shave* themselves in such a state?

Second, that of Dylan Thomas, in his Notes on the Art of Poetry*:*

Read the poems you like reading. Don't bother whether they're important, or if they'll live. What does it matter what poetry *is*, after all? If you want a definition of poetry, say 'Poetry is what makes me laugh or cry or yawn, what makes my toenails twinkle, what makes me want to do this or that or nothing', and let it go at that. All that matters about poetry is the enjoyment of it, however tragic it may be. All that matters is the eternal movement behind it, the vast undercurrent of human grief, folly, pretension, exaltation, or ignorance, however unlofty the intention of the poem.

You can tear a poem apart to see what makes it technically tick, and say to yourself, when the works are laid out before you, the vowels, the consonants, the rhymes and rhythms, 'Yes, this is *it*. This is why the poem moves me so. It is because of the craftsmanship.' But you're back again where you began. You're back with the mystery of having been moved by words. The best craftsmanship always leaves holes and gaps in the works of the poem so that something that is *not* in the poem can creep, crawl, flash or thunder in.

The joy and function of poetry is, and was, the celebration of man, which is also the celebration of God.

But even poetry is not invariably beneficial. William Wordsworth was described by the local innkeeper:

Takin' his family out in a string and niver geeing the deariest bit of notice to 'em; standin' by hisself and stoppin' behind agapin', with his jaws workin' the whoal time; but niver no crackin' wi' 'em, nor no pleasure in 'em – a desolate-minded man, ye kna' – it was potry as did it.

Roger North on Sir Matthew Hale (1609–1676), Lord Chief Justice of England:

This great man was most unfortunate in his family; for he married his own servant maid and then, for an excuse, said there was no wisdom below the girdle. All his sons died in the sink of lewdness and debauchery.

Here are a few items extracted from the catalogue of the sale (twenty-sixth day)
of the Bullock Museum in 1819, at which were sold a number of objects formerly
the property of Napoleon and taken after Waterloo.

Lot

70: A Drawer from a small Canteen, containing a Tumbler-glass, two
small Tumblers for Spirits, an Egg-cup of China; Pepper, Salt-box,
and Mustard-pot, all of silver, having the contents as left by the
Emperor at his last breakfast before the battle of Waterloo still in
them. [£7.8.0, purchaser not listed]

72: A Silver Déjeuné [sic] plate, used in ordinary in the carriage.
(£4.4.0, Lee)

78: A Glass Spirit-bottle, with the Rum left by the Emperor still in it.
[Chamberlain]

THE EMPEROR'S PERSONAL WARDROBE, TAKEN IN THE CARRIAGE

80: His ordinary travelling Cap of Green Velvet. [£5.6.0, Chamberlain]

82: A pair of White Silk Stockings, with the Imperial Crest on the
clock (a crown). [£2.2.0, Chamberlain]

90: A very fine Cambric Pocket-handkerchief, handsomely embroid-
ered with the N in the corner. [£2.2.0, Capt. Campbell-Brooke]

95: A pair of Braces. [£0.16.0, Clift]

96: A Diaper Towel, marked N-10. [£1.2.0, Do.]

98: Another marked L. and crown, which probably belonged to Louis
XVIII. [£1.0.0, Riddell]

99: Flesh-brush. [£0.15.0, Trevallion]

100: Green silk Pincushion, filled with sweet-scented wood. [£1.1.0,
Bailey]

105: Set of Chessmen in a round wooden box, used by the Emperor in
the Russian campaign. [£2.9.0, Lincoln]

**The two massive Silver Articles of personal convenience, used in
the carriage, will be disposed of by Private Contract.**

[£31.10.0, The Prince Regent]

Do these last, one longs to know, still form part of the Royal Collection?

*[I have since heard that they do. HRH The Prince of Wales has himself confirmed
to me that they are at Windsor, where they are kept in a cupboard in the Grand
Vestibule, on the way to the Waterloo Chamber.]*

Three of G. K. Chesterton's 'Variations on an Air', composed, he tells us, On Having to Appear in a Pageant as Old King Cole:

AFTER TENNYSON:

Cole, that unwearied prince of Colchester,
Growing more gay with age and with long days
Deeper in laughter and desire of life,
As that Virginian climber on our walls
Flames scarlet with the fading of the year,
Called for his wassail and that other weed
Virginian also, from the western woods
Where English Raleigh checked the boast of Spain;
And lighting joy with joy, and piling up
Pleasure as crown for pleasure, bade me bring
Those three, the minstrels whose emblazoned coats
Shone with the oyster-shells of Colchester;
And these three played, and playing grew more fain
Of mirth and music; till the heathen came,
And the King slept beside the northern sea.

AFTER BROWNING:

Who smoke-snorts toasts o' My Lady Nicotine,
Kicks stuffing out of Pussyfoot, bids his trio
Stick up their Stradivarii (that's the plural)
Or near enough, my fatheads; *nimium*
Vicina Cremonae; (that's a bit too near.)
Is there some stockfish fails to understand?
Catch hold o' the notion, bellow and blurt back 'Cole'?
Must I bawl lessons from a horn-book, howl,
Cat-call the cat-gut 'fiddles'? Fiddlesticks!

AFTER SWINBURNE:

In the time of old sin without sadness,
    And golden with wastage of gold,
Like the gods that grow old in their gladness
    Was the King that was glad, growing old:
And with sound of loud lyres from his palace
    The voice of his oracles spoke,
And the lips that were red from his chalice
    Were splendid with smoke.

When the weed was as flame for a token
  And the wine was as blood for a sign;
And upheld in his hands and unbroken
  The fountains of fire and of wine.
And a song without speech, without singer,
  Stung the soul of a thousand in three,
As the flesh of the earth has to sting her,
  The soul of the sea.

Since I started working with Classic FM, I have had to read an awful lot of musical programme notes; and I find myself feeling more and more in sympathy with George Bernard Shaw – a rare experience with me – in his detestation of them. Just imagine, he writes, if Hamlet's great soliloquy were to be subjected to similar treatment:

'Shakespear, dispensing with the customary exordium, announces his subject at once in the infinitive, in which mood it is presently repeated after a short connecting passage in which, brief as it is, we recognize the alternative and negative forms on which so much of the significance of repetition depends. Here we reach a colon; and a pointed pository phrase, in which the accent falls decisively on the relative pronoun, brings us to the first full stop.'

I break off here because, to confess the truth, my grammar is giving out. But I want to know whether it is just that a literary critic should be forbidden to make his living in this way on pain of being interviewed by two doctors and a magistrate, and hailed off to Bedlam forthwith; whilst the more a musical critic does it, the deeper the veneration he inspires.

The will of Samuel Jeffery, purser of His Majesty's Ship Amphion, *1810:*

Considering well the perils and dangers of the sea, viz. that a chance shot may kill the devil, to my friends Jack Dalling, Joe Cape and Tom Boardman the sum of £10 between them, to pay for a good dinner, which I wish them to have in remembrance of me, and request they will drink a speedy and safe passage to me to the other world. My rings &c. to my brother William Henry Jeffery, to do with them as his own saucy fancy may direct: I particularly wish him to get a bit of my hair (from whatever part of me I don't care) to put in a locket; and my grand request is that when it shall please God to call me aloft, that some good fellow will stow my piciolo corpo into my great chest. If I die strait, they will, I know, have occasion to force me in; but, never mind, I'll promise not to sing out; and then, after securing it well, to keep me safe from all intruders, launch me overboard, in good deep water, with plenty of ballast. And now as I have nothing more to give, bequeath or request, I will finish by putting my hand and seal to this, my royal will, 10 o'clock, 10th January, 1810.

In the heaven of God I hope for (call him X)
There is marriage and giving in marriage and transient sex
For those who will cast the body's vest aside
Soon, but are not yet wholly rarefied
And still embrace. For X is never annoyed
Or shocked; has read his Jung and knows his Freud,
He gives you time in heaven to do as you please,
To climb love's gradual ladder by slow degrees,
Gently to rise from sense to soul, to ascend
To a world of timeless joy, world without end.

Here on the gates of pearl there hangs no sign
Limiting cakes and ale, forbidding wine.
No weakness here is hidden, no vice unknown.
Sin is a sickness to be cured, outgrown.
With the help of a god who can laugh, an unsolemn god
Who smiles at old wives' tales of iron rod
And fiery hell, a god who's more at ease
With bawds and Falstaffs than with pharisees.

Here the lame learn to leap, the blind to see.
Tyrants are taught to be humble, slaves to be free.
Fools become wise, and wise men cease to be bores,
Here bishops learn from the lips of back-street whores,
And white men follow black-faced angels' feet
Through fields of orient and immortal wheat.

Villon, Lautrec and Baudelaire are here.
Here Swift forgets his anger, Poe his fear.
Napoleon rests; Columbus, journeys done,
Has reached his new Atlantis, found his sun.
Verlaine and Dylan Thomas drink together,
Marx talks to Plato, Byron wonders whether
There's some mistake. Wordsworth has found a hill
That's home. Here Chopin plays the piano still.
Wren plans ethereal domes; and Renoir paints
Young girls as ripe as fruit but not yet saints.

And X, of whom no coward is afraid,
Who's friend consulted, not fierce king obeyed,
Who bears the unspoken thought, the prayer unprayed,
Who expects not even the learned to understand
His universe, extends a prodigal hand,
Full of forgiveness, over his promised land.

A. S. J. Tessimond

For some strange reason murder has always seemed more respectable than fornication. Few people are shocked when they hear God described as the God of Battles; but what an outcry there would be if anyone spoke of him as the God of Brothels.

Aldous Huxley,
Grey Eminence

Tony Quinton sends me the following little masterpiece, inspired, he tells me, by a reading of the Annual Report of St Hilda's College, Oxford, with numerous similar pieces from ageing alumnae:

The Palace
N'Gommh
Abu Dubba

Dear Mrs Moore,

It was a great thrill when the St Hilda's 'Report and Chronicle' arrived at the Palace here the other day. It was very good to hear so much of what was going on in the college. It was most interesting to compare what other people who have gone down have been doing with my life in the Middle East – all those teachers and librarians and social workers and so on.

After Schools I hung about a bit doing nothing in particular and because my degree in French was no great shakes I was very relieved when a cousin of Mummy's fixed me up with a job in the cataloguing department of Christie's. The work was a bit monotonous, but interesting people came in and out. One day very much so, a glamorous dark man in lovely clothes who was really looking at jewelled scabbards but seemed to be interested in my Herefordshire pot lids. Sonny and I went out a few times and in quite a short time he proposed. Daddy was too ill to come to the wedding here and Mummy felt she had to stay with him, so it was a lonely start.

All the same, I soon came to get on pretty well with most of my colleagues in the harem. The main wife, Oufa, is his cousin, a rather large lady who doesn't do much and who I've rather steered clear of. (In a way she is as formidable as Mrs Prestwich, but much bigger.) There are two other Europeans – Hortense, who is French and always exquisitely turned out, and Wanda, a Ukrainian, quite nice and terrifically strong but unfortunately she can't speak a word of any language I can understand.

It's a quiet life on the whole – no servant problem to worry about. Sonny liked my idea of organizing self-help groups for blind widows (there seem to be an awful lot of them!). I wanted to call the scheme A Blind Bit of Good, but they don't use the words in that way.

The big event for us is of course the Khnouf, or summons. This means that Sonny wants one to go to him. One feels one is for the high jump, like being called for by Mrs Bennett, well not exactly but you know what I mean. There is a huge, black, well actually *eunuch* called Zamoun who oils and prepares the wives for the Prince's

221

bedchamber. Not very nice really but I suppose one is reasonably safe.

I have two sons who will be going to school in England in due course. Sonny, by the way, despite his name, is really an absolute Shiite, very strict, except for drinking. I do hope I shall be able to drop in to some gathering at St Hilda's before too long.

Yours sincerely,

Heather Clavering-Thorpe (1969–72)
Princess Anouf Hama'a al Abnoim Hazgallah

There is a remarkable plaque in the parish church of St Mary, Battersea, to one Edward Wynter, who died in 1686. A sculpture in relief illustrates two of his more remarkable achievements:

> Alone unarmed a Tigre he opprest
> And crushed to death ye Monster of a Beast.
> Thrice-twenty mounted Moors he overthrew
> Singly on foot, some wounded, some he slew,
> Dispers'd ye rest; what more could Samson do?

The inscription fails to mention that Wynter was in fact an utterly unscrupulous adventurer, who for three years (1665–8) was virtual dictator of Madras, in defiance of the King and of the East India Company who had sent him there.

Other encounters with tigers were less happy in their outcome. In the churchyard of Malmesbury Abbey a gravestone is inscribed:

In Memory of

Hannah TWYNNOY

Who died October 23rd, 1703

Aged 33 years.

> In bloom of life
> She's snatched from hence,
> She had not room
> To make defence;
> For Tyger fierce
> Took Life away,
> And here she lies
> In a bed of Clay,
> Until the Resurrection Day.

A curious fate for a Wiltshire girl.

Dominic de Grunne has sent me an article by 'La Reynière' in Le Monde, 18
January 1992, about the Grand Hôtel in Paris. I knew that it was where poor,
mad Empress Charlotte of Mexico stayed in August 1866 when she returned to
Europe in a last desperate attempt to persuade Napoleon III to send troops to the
defence of her beleaguered husband Maximilian; but I had forgotten – if indeed I
ever knew – that it was also where Emile Zola's Nana died of smallpox, in
Room 401.

It was in the bar that André Gide, Pierre Louÿs and Paul Valéry (in that order)
improvised, line by line, the quatrain:

> Gloire aux barbes de fer nocturnement éparses,
> Effarant leurs poils morts dans les bras étendus
> Les sols, de corps jonchés au choc des métatarses
> Ont vaporisé l'or des sables épandus[1]

Gide supplying both the first line and the last.

The hotel also provided the venue, on 26 February 1903, for the first luncheon of
the Académie Goncourt. But surely one of its most brilliant evenings must have
been that of 6 February 1865 when, at the instigation of the celebrated naturalist
Geoffroy Saint-Hilaire, it held its 'Grand Banquet Hippophagique'. The menu
was the following:

Vermicelle au bouillon de cheval

Saucisson et charcuterie de cheval

Cheval bouilli, cheval à la mode

Ragoût de cheval, filet de cheval aux champignons

Pommes sautées à la graisse de cheval

Salade à l'huile de cheval

Gâteau au rhum à la moelle de cheval

– washed down, it need hardly be said, with copious quantities of Cheval Blanc.
Edmond de Goncourt described the meat as being 'aqueuse et d'un rouge
noirâtre'. The chef's name was Balzac.

---

[1] *I tried to translate this, but gave up. Any translation that anybody would like to send*
me, if sufficiently up to snuff, will be printed in next year's Cracker.

In Flavia's eye is every grace,
She's handsome as she could be:
With Jacob's beauty in her face
And Esau's where it should be.

Lord Chesterfield

Bonus

It is not generally known that among the works of Rupert Brooke unpublished at the time of his death was an unfinished fragment of a novel, The Death of John Rump. *It ends with an epilogue in verse, set in heaven. Here is its conclusion:*

FIRST SERAPH *(pointing downwards):* I see a speck, immediately below.

MANY LITTLE CHERUBS: Bravo! Bravo! Bravo!

SECOND SERAPH: I see it too. A black speck. Very far!

CHERUBS: Huzza! Huzza! Huzza!

THIRD SERAPH *(excitedly):* 'Tis him! 'tis him! upon his upward way!

CHERUBS: Hooray! Hooray! Hooray!

GOD *(rising):*   I do espy him like a fretful midge,
The while his wide and alternating vans
Winnow the buxom air. With flight serene
He wings amidst the watery Pleiades;
Now Leo feels his passage, and the Twins;
Orion now, and that unwieldy girth
Hight Scorpio; as when a trader bound
For Lamda or the isle of Mogador,
Freighted with ambergris and stilbium,
And what rich odours . . .

(The remaining 127 lines are lost in the increasing hubbub. Enter, from below on the left, JOHN RUMP *in top hat, frock coat etc., bearing an umbrella. He stands impassive in the middle)*

GOD: John Rump, of Balham, Leeds and Canterbury,
Why are you wearing hideous black clothes?

RUMP: Because I am an English gentleman.

GOD: John Rump, we gave you life and all its wonder.
What splendid tidings have you got to tell?

RUMP: God, I have been an English gentleman.

GOD: Infinite splendour has been in your power;
John Rump, what have you got to show for life?

RUMP: God, I have been an English gentleman.

GOD *(rising angrily):* Was it for this we sent you to the world,
And gave you life and knowledge, made you man,
Crowned you with glory? You could have worked and
laughed,
Sung, loved, and kissed, made all the world a dream,
Found infinite beauty in a leaf or word . . .
. . . Perish eternally, you and your hat!

RUMP *(not wincing):* You long-haired aesthetes, get you out of heaven!
I, John Rump, I, an English Gentleman,
Do not believe in you and all your gushing.
I am John Rump, this is my hat, and this
My umbrella. I stand here for sense,
Invincible, inviolable, eternal,
For safety, regulations, paving-stones,
Street-lamps, police, and bijou-residences
Semi-detached. I stand for Sanity,
Comfort, Content, Prosperity, Top hats,
Alcohol, Collars, Meat. Tariff Reform
Means higher wages and more work for all.

(As he speaks, GOD *and the seraphic multitude grow faint, mistier and mistier, become ineffectually wavering shadows, and vanish. The floor of Heaven rocks . . . the thrones and glassy sea . . . all has vanished.* JOHN RUMP *remains, still and expressionless, leaning on his umbrella, growing larger and larger, infinitely menacing, filling the universe, blotting out the stars . . .)*

CURTAIN

A
Christmas
Cracker

1997

From the Notebooks of Samuel Butler:

The little Strangs say the 'good words', as they call them, before going to bed, aloud and at their father's knee, or rather in the pit of his stomach. One of them was lately heard to say, 'Forgive us our Christmases, as we forgive them that Christmas against us.'

I'm reminded of a little quatrain that I noted down myself a year or two ago – stupidly, without noting the name of the author – on the increasing popularity of the secular Christmas card:

> 'Noel!', the festive robin cried,
> When he the heavenly babe espied,
> But Santa said 'Enough of that!'
> And with a yule log squashed him flat.

[The mystery of the origin of this verse has now been solved: its authorship has been proudly claimed by Leo Cooper.]

Over the main entrance of Cardinal Chigi's Villa Cetinale, at Sovicille in Tuscany, there is a marble plaque carrying the following inscription:

QUISQUIS HUC ACCEDIS

QUOD TIBI HORRENDUM VIDETUR

MIHI AMOENUM EST

SI DILECTAT MANEAS

SI TAEDET ABEAS

UTRUMQUE GRATUM

which could be translated:

YOU WHO COME HERE WHOEVER YOU ARE

WHAT MAY SEEM HORRIBLE TO YOU

IS FINE FOR ME

IF YOU LIKE IT STAY

IF IT BORES YOU GO

I COULDN'T CARE LESS

In last year's Cracker I included three parodies on 'Old King Cole' by G. K. Chesterton, in the style of Tennyson, Browning and Swinburne. People seem to have enjoyed them, so here are two more by the same author.

AFTER YEATS:

Of an Old King in a story
    From the grey sea-folk I have heard,
Whose heart was no more broken
    Than the wings of a bird.

As soon as the moon was silver
    And the thin stars began,
He took his pipe and his tankard
    Like an old peasant man.

And three tall shadows were with him
    And came at his command;
And played before him for ever
    The fiddles of fairyland.

And he died in the young summer
    Of the world's desire;
Before our hearts were broken
    Like sticks in a fire.

AND AFTER WHITMAN:

Me clairvoyant,
Me conscious of you, old camarado,
Needing no telescope, lorgnette, field-glass, opera-glass, myopic
    pince-nez,
Me piercing two thousand years with eye naked and not ashamed,
The crown cannot hide you from me;
Musty old feudal-heraldic trappings cannot hide you from me,
I perceive that you drink.
(I am drinking with you. I am as drunk as you are.)
I see you are inhaling tobacco, puffing, smoking, spitting
(I do not object to your spitting),
You prophetic of American largeness,
You anticipating the broad masculine manners of these States;
I see in you also there are movements, tremors, tears, desire for the
    melodious,
I salute your three violinists, endlessly making vibrations,

233

Rigid, relentless, capable of going on for ever;
They play my accompaniment; but I shall take no notice of any
    accompaniment;
I myself am a complete orchestra.
So long.

In June 1991 the Royal College of Art exhibited, on an open terrace immediately opposite the east side of the Albert Hall, a sculpture by Ben Panting entitled Honi Soit qui Mal y Pense *and depicting, in remorseless detail and at least twelve times life-size, the act of copulation. Astonishingly enough, almost everybody walked straight past, not noticing it at all. The police, on the other hand, spotted it and demanded its immediate removal; a demand which Jocelyn Stevens – then Rector of the College – very properly refused. A few days later he received a copy of a letter addressed to Mr Panting, which so surprised him that he immediately telephoned the sender to confirm its authenticity. He was assured that the letter was genuine, and the request a serious one.*

British Safety Council
Chancellor's Road
London w6

11 June 1991

Dear Mr Panting,

Firstly may we congratulate you on the fine piece of art presently being exhibited outside the RCA. *Honi Soit qui Mal y Pense* really is a fine depiction of the pure art of penetration.

The purpose of writing to you is to ask you if we could use this sculpture as a centre piece for our annual campaign, National Condom Week.

Now in its fifth year, National Condom Week is about the positive promotion of the Condom, and safe sex, now of paramount import- ance in these days of ever increasing occurrences of sexually trans- mitted diseases and the HIV virus. We would therefore propose either to attach a condom to your sculpture, thereby enhancing the very real nature of safe sex, or alternatively we would welcome any way you may be able to help us . . .

Yours sincerely,

[sgd.] Victoria Brown

Manager, Press PR and Awards
For and on behalf of James Tye, Director General

Memorable opening sentences of books? Most people, if asked, tend to quote the first sentence of Rose Macaulay's The Towers of Trebizond:

> 'Take my camel dear,' said my aunt Dot, as she climbed down from the animal on her return from High Mass.

Some years ago, however, Teddy Hodgkin put up another candidate. The Life of Bishop Reginald Heber *(author of* From Greenland's Icy Mountains) *by George Smith, CIE, LLD, begins:*

> Two generations have passed away since the death of Reginald Heber in his bath at Trichinopoly.

Heber won the Newdigate Prize with a poem called 'Palestine', about which his biographer writes:

> On mounting the rostrum to recite his poem, he was struck by seeing two young ladies of Jewish extraction, sitting in a conspicuous part of the theatre. The recollection of some lines which reflect severely on their nation flashed across his mind, and he resolved to spare their feelings by softening the passage which he feared would give them pain, as he proceeded; but it was impossible to communicate this intention to his brother, who was sitting behind him as prompter and who, on the attempt being made, immediately checked him, so that he was forced to recall the lines as they were originally written.

The lines in question must have been the following:

> While Israel's sons, by scorpion curses driven,
> Outcasts of earth, and reprobate of heaven,
> Through the wide world in friendless exile stray,
> Remorse and shame sole comrades of their way,
> With dumb despair their country's wrong behold,
> And, dead to glory, only burn for gold.

A few lines later, however, Heber becomes positively Zionist:

> And shall not Israel's sons exulting come,
> Hail the glad beam, and claim their ancient home?
> On David's throne shall David's offspring reign,
> And the dry bones be warm with life again.

– which must have come as a great relief to the Jewish ladies. In his comments on other races and religions the Bishop, it must be said, emerges as being neither perceptive nor profound. The following quatrain is taken from his poem 'An Evening Walk in Bengal':

> Upon her deck, 'mid charcoal gleams,
> The Moslem's savoury supper steams,
> While all apart beneath the wood
> The Hindoo cooks his simpler food.

About suffering they were never wrong,
The Old Masters: how well they understood
Its human position; how it takes place
While someone else is eating or opening a window or just walking
    dully along;
How, when the aged are reverently, passionately waiting
For the miraculous birth, there always must be
Children who did not specially want it to happen, skating
On a pond at the edge of the wood:
They never forget
That even the dreadful martyrdom must run its course
Anyhow in a corner, some untidy spot
Where the dogs go on with their doggy life and the torturer's horse
Scratches its innocent behind on a tree.
In Brueghel's *Icarus*, for instance: how everything turns away
Quite leisurely from the disaster; the ploughman may
Have heard the splash, the forsaken cry,
But for him it was not an important failure; the sun shone
As it had to on the white legs disappearing into the green
Water; and the expensive delicate ship that must have seen
Something amazing, a boy falling out of the sky,
Had somewhere to get to and sailed calmly on.

                                W. H. Auden

This inspired description of dolphins comes from the pen of – who else? – Paddy Leigh Fermor. It is to be found in his Mani, *to which we gave our Duff Cooper Prize in 1959.*

Soon the delighted cry of '*Delphinia!*' went up: a school of dolphins were gambolling half a mile further out to sea. They seemed to have spotted us at the same moment for, in a second, half a dozen were tearing their way towards us, all surfacing in the same parabola and plunging together as though they were in some invisible harness. Soon they were careering alongside and round the bows and under the bowsprit, glittering mussel-blue on top, fading at the sides through gun-metal dune-like markings to pure white, streamlined and gleaming from their elegant beaks to the clean-cut flukes of their tails. They were beautiful abstractions of speed, energy, power and ecstasy, leaping out of the water and plunging and spiralling and vanishing like swift shadows, each soon to materialize again and sail into the air in another great loop, so fast that they seemed to draw the sea after them and shake it off in mid-air, to plunge forward again tearing two great frothing bow-waves with their beaks; diving down again, falling behind and criss-crossing under the keel, and deviating and returning. Sometimes they flung themselves out of the sea with the insane abandon, in reverse, of a suicide from a skyscraper; up, up, until they hung poised in mid-air, shaking in a muscular convulsion from beak to tail as though resolved to abandon their element for ever. But gravity, as though hauling on an oblique fishing-line, dragged them forward and down again into their rifled and bubbling green tunnels. The headlong speed through the water filled the air with a noise of rending and searing. Each leap into the air called forth a chorus of gasps, each plunge a sigh . . .

Four years ago, I was sailing through the Outer Cyclades in the late afternoon of a long and dreamlike day. The steep flank of Sikinos, tinkling with goat bells and aflutter with birds, rose up to starboard and, close to port, the sheer cliffs of Nereid-haunted Pholegandros. A few bars of unlikely midsummer cloud lay across the west. All at once the sun's rim appeared blood-red under the lowest bar, hemming the clouds with gold wire and sending a Japanese flag of widening sunbeams, alternating with expanding spokes of deeper sky, into the air for miles and spreading rose petals and sulphur green across this silk lake. Then, some distance off, a dolphin sailed into the air; then another and yet another, until a small company were flying and diving and chasing each other and hovering in mid-air in static semi-circles, gambolling and curvetting and almost playing leap-frog, trying to stand on tiptoe, pirouetting and jumping over the sinking sun. All we could hear was an occasional splash, and so smooth was the water that one could see spreading rings when they swooped below the surface. The sea became a meadow, and these antics like the last game of children on a lawn before going to bed. Leaning spellbound over the bulwarks and in the rigging, we watched them in silence. All at once, on a sudden decision, they vanished.

'*Kala einai ta delfinia*,' the captain said when they had gone. 'They're good.'

Here now is an illuminating insight into the ways of British Colonial government, at least as it was half a century ago. On 8 June 1936, Mr R. V. Vernon of the Colonial Office drafted a Memorandum, of which the following is an extract:

The sentence in the draft Report under discussion was as follows: 'Mr Ormsby Gore[1] dwelt upon the strategic and economic importance of the Colonies.' Sir Edward Harding[2] thought it was very unwise to say anything about the strategic importance of the Colonies. If anyone were to look at a map of the Colonies he might find out where Singapore was, and who could say what that would lead to? He proposed to strike out the word 'strategic'. Mr Vernon agreed.

Sir Harry Batterbee[3] thought that it was very dangerous to refer to the economic importance of the Colonies. Any such reference would direct the mind of the reader to the claims of Germany for the restoration of her past colonial empire upon purely economic grounds. He thought that the words should be omitted. Mr Vernon agreed.

Sir Rupert Howorth[4] did not like emphasis being laid on the importance of the Colonies. We were already to a large extent the object of envy and suspicion of the world on account of our possession of colonies. The best line for us to take now was to minimize their importance, and even to underrate them. He suggested that the word 'importance' should be omitted. Mr Vernon agreed.

The sentence in the draft now read: 'Mr Ormsby Gore dwelt upon the Colonies'. Mr Archer[5] thought that this was a rather unhappy expression in that it suggested a lingering, continued exposition of the colonial aspect of inter-imperial affairs, which might very easily provoke jealousy on the part of the Dominions. Mr Vernon pointed out that the report would probably be read by a large number of agents of foreign governments who might be imperfectly acquainted with the English language. There was a grave risk that they would interpret the words 'Mr Ormsby Gore dwelt upon the Colonies' as meaning 'Mr Ormsby Gore dwelt in the Colonies'. This would not be true. He suggested the substitution of the words 'referred to'. Sir Edward Harding pointed out that these words had already appeared in every sentence of the draft Report which had so far been passed, and he thought it would be a

---

[1] Later Lord Harlech. Colonial Secretary, 1936–8.
[2] Permanent Under-Secretary, Dominions Office.
[3] Assistant Under-Secretary of State, Dominions Office.
[4] Administrative Assistant Secretary, Imperial Conferences.
[5] As above.

good thing to find another expression this time. Sir Harry Batterbee suggested the words 'alluded to'. Mr Vernon agreed.

This sentence thus revised read: 'Mr Ormsby Gore alluded to the Colonies'. Sir Rupert Howorth enquired whether it would not really be better to leave the sentence out altogether. If the Report merely stated that Mr Ormsby Gore alluded to the Colonies, it might excite suspicion on the part of foreign readers that the real gist of his remarks had been of a quite different character, and that this was nothing more than a screen or a disguise. Sir Harry Batterbee pointed out that Mr Ormsby Gore's name would in any case appear as one of those present, and that as he was Secretary of State for the Colonies it might probably arouse some jealousy in the minds of Dominion statesmen if they considered that he had talked about the Dominions just as if they were colonies. It therefore seemed wiser to leave the sentence in. Mr Vernon agreed, but suggested that the addition of the word 'furtively' before 'alluded to' might be an improvement. This was negatived without a division.

My dear friend Martine de Courcel recently sent me the following verse, originally written for Madame de Verrue, but which she describes as an 'epitaphe d'une aventurière bien née et de petite vertu':

> Ci-gît dans une paix profonde
> Cette dame de volupté
> Qui, pour plus grande sûreté,
> Fit son paradis en ce monde.

which in turn reminded me of lines once quoted to me by the much-missed Gérard André:

> Comme disait Colbert à Monsieur de Louvois,
> Que n'ai-je baisé plus, quand baiser je pouvois?

O Lord, thou knowest how busy I must be this day: if I forget thee, do not thou forget me.

That was the prayer of Sir Jacob Astley, Sergeant-Major-General of Foot to the army of Charles I at the battle of Edgehill on 13 October 1642. His prayer was granted – up to a point. He was slightly wounded, but was fully recovered in time to take part in the unsuccessful siege of Gloucester the following August. Field-Marshal Wavell points out in his (alas) unpublished commonplace book – not to be confused with his superb anthology Other Men's Flowers – *that:*

> there are some good prayers before battle – Sir Jacob Astley's before Edgehill, Drake's before Cadiz, Wingate's on his entry into Burma and others.

Drake's prayer runs as follows:

> O Lord God, when thou givest thy servants to endeavour any great matter, grant us also to know that it is not the beginning, but the continuing of the same until it be thoroughly finished, that yieldeth the true glory.

And Wingate's:

> Knowing the vanity of man's effort and the confusion of his purpose, let us pray that God may accept our services and direct our endeavours, so that when we shall have done all we shall see the fruits of our labours and be satisfied.

But Falstaff's, before the battle of Shrewsbury, is the simplest of all:

> I would 'twere bed time, Hal, and all well.

All the trees they are so high,
   The leaves they are so green,
The day is past and gone, sweet heart,
   That you and I have seen.
      It is cold winter's night,
      You and I must bide alone:
         Whilst my pretty lad is young
         And is growing.

O father, father dear,
   Great wrong to me is done,
That I should married be this day,
   Before the set of sun.
      O the wind on the thatch.
      Here, and I alone must weep
         Whilst my pretty lad is young
         And is growing.

My daughter, daughter dear,
   If better be, more fit,
I'll send him to the court awhile,
   To point his pretty wit.
      But the snow, snowflakes fall,
      O and I am chill as dead:
         Whilst my pretty lad is young
         And is growing.

To let the lovely ladies know
   They may not touch and taste,
I'll bind a bunch of ribbons red
   About his little waist.
      But the raven hoarsely croaks,
      And I shiver in my bed;
         Whilst my pretty lad is young
         And is growing.

I married was, alas,
   A lady high to be,
In court and stall and stately hall
   And bower of tapestry.
      But the bell did only knell,
      And I shuddered as one cold:
         When I wed the pretty lad
         Not done growing.

At fourteen he wedded was,
    A father at fifteen,
At sixteen's face was white as milk,
    And then his grave was green;
        And the daisies were outspread,
        And buttercups of gold,
            O'er my pretty lad so young
            Now ceased growing.

                                Anon.

I'm in a quandary about an MS play by Robert Nichols called *Komusu*, about a set of English people in Japan, date 1922. I've read it twice, and find it terribly bogus, and crammed with sins against good taste and common sense. *What* am I to say about it? As for bogus, there's a background of silly symbols, for instance a singing insect called an 'ammakirigirisu', which provides a running obbligato to every turn of the plot by dint of crescendos, sudden silences, and abrupt interrogatory squawks. Halfway through the play the creature is let out of its cage and turned loose in the garden, so that one hopes one has heard the last of it – but no, it remains in the neighbourhood and keeps up its uncanny interest in, and knowledge of, and commentary on, the doings of the characters to the end. For common sense, there's the most elaborate seduction scene ever devised, with every movement of the gay Lothario's hands over the nape, arms, bosom, etc. of the transcendently beautiful and altogether flawless heroine minutely described in stage-directions – all this apparently in total darkness, as the electric light has failed owing to an earthquake tremor. For good taste, when some weeks later the heroine tells the Lothario that her husband, Eliot by name, is upset at learning that she is with child, he tells her that it's no wonder Eliot is resentful at finding his rival's false teeth in his orange. (This is the culmination of a laboured structure of apologue about stolen oranges, with which I won't trouble you.) I'm sure you'll sympathize with me, as Robert thinks the play is a masterpiece, and is very sensitive.

Elsewhere, he writes:

My only job has been the proofs of John Hayward's index – quite satisfactory except that there seemed to be an unnecessary number of double entries. This wouldn't be worth mentioning, except that it reminded me of an amusing *triple* entry that I once saw quoted from the index of a book on British Guiana.

> Up a creek in Demerara:
> Creek in Demerara, Up a:
> Demerara, Up a creek in:

It might almost be in *Hiawatha*.

[*Debo Devonshire writes of Eddie Marsh: 'My father-in-law took pity on him after he had been knocked down by a taxi in St James's St in the war and asked him to stay for a while till he felt better. He stayed for 18 months. My sisters-in-law and I were young and impatient and were driven nearly mad by him. He turned on the news at 9.0 every night & then went straight to sleep – but woke up if we turned it off.'*]

See the mothers in the park,
Ugly creatures chiefly;
Someone must have loved them once,
In the dark, and briefly.

Anon.

In the 1972 Cracker *I included a few holorhymes – lines which have the same sound, but different meanings. For some reason the French seem to be rather better at them than we are:*

L'esquimau réjoui à mi-voix le retient:
'Laisse qui mord et jouis! Ami, vois l'heure, tiens!'

In his Sortilèges du Verbe, *Matyla Ghika quotes a splendid one:*

Dans ces meubles laqués, rideaux et dais moroses,
Danse, aime, bleu laquais, ris d'oser des mots roses!
Par le bois du djinn, ou s'entasse de l'effroi,
Parle! Bois du gin, ou cent tasses de lait froid.

And another, which he tells us was whispered into his ear by Marcel Hérault during a grim dinner-party:

Eprise, hélas! Eve nue
Offrit son bec à Satan;
Et prise, et lasse, et venue
Au frisson, bécasse, attend . . .

Yet another is attributed to my old friend Sacha de Menziarly by Jean François Deniau in his Mémoires de sept vies:

Et ma blême araignée, ogre illogique et las,
Aimable, aime à régner au gris logis qu'elle a.

He adds, for good measure, a pretty palindrome:

Luce le valet te lave le cul.

From Helen Waddell's marvellous Lyrics from the Chinese, *here is a poem written, she tells us, in 769 BC. The author is not named, so presumably unknown.*

My lord is gone away to serve the King.
The pigeons homing at the set of sun
Are side by side upon the courtyard wall,
And far away I hear the herdsmen call
The goats upon the hill when day is done.
But I, I know not when he will come home.
      I live the days alone.

My lord is gone away to serve the King.
I hear a pigeon stirring in the nest
And in the field a pheasant crying late.
She has not far to go to find her mate.
There is a hunger will not let me rest.
The days have grown to months, and months to years,
      And I have no more tears.

Two years – and two Crackers – ago I transcribed a lovely French sonnet of just fourteen words. Thanks to my friend Jane Rylands, I'm now able to include an English one with the same number. The author is Frank Sidgwick; the title is 'The Aeronaut to his Lady'.

I
Through
Blue
Sky
Fly
To
You.
Why?
Sweet
Love,
Feet
Move
So
Slow!

Edward Gibbon tells us – in a passage which I have very slightly abridged – what he believes to be the truth about our Patron Saint:

George, from his parents or his education surnamed the Cappadocian, was born in Epiphania in Cilicia, in a fuller's shop. From this obscure and servile origin he raised himself by the talents of a parasite; and the patrons whom he assiduously flattered procured for their worthless dependant a lucrative commission, or contract, to supply the army with bacon. His employment was mean; he rendered it infamous. He accumulated wealth by the basest arts of fraud and corruption; but his malversations were so notorious, that George was compelled to escape from the pursuits of justice. From the love, or the ostentation, of learning, he collected a valuable library of history, rhetoric, philosophy and theology; and the choice of the prevailing faction promoted George of Cappadocia to the throne of Athanasius. The entrance of the new archbishop was that of a barbarian conqueror; and each moment of his reign was polluted by cruelty and avarice. The catholics of Alexandria and Egypt were abandoned to a tyrant, qualified by nature and education to exercise the office of persecution; but he oppressed with an impartial hand the various inhabitants of his extensive diocese. The primate of Egypt assumed the pomp and insolence of his lofty station; but he still betrayed the vices of his base and servile extraction. The merchants of Alexandria were impoverished by the unjust and almost universal monopoly, which he acquired, of nitre, salt, paper, funerals, etc.: and the spiritual father of a great people condescended to practise the vile and pernicious arts of an informer.

Under the reign of Constantius he was expelled by the fury, or rather by the justice, of the people; and George, with two of his obsequious ministers, Count Diodorus, and Dracontius, master of the mint, were ignominiously dragged in chains to the public prison. At the end of twenty-four days the prison was forced open by the rage of a superstitious multitude, impatient of the tedious forms of judicial proceedings. The enemies of gods and men expired under their cruel insults; the lifeless bodies of the archbishop and his associates were carried in triumph through the streets on the back of a camel and were thrown into the sea. The meritorious death of the archbishop obliterated the memory of his life. The odious stranger, disguising every circumstance of time and place, assumed the mask of a martyr, a saint, and a Christian hero; and the infamous George of Cappadocia has been transformed into the renowned St George of England, the patron of arms, of chivalry and of the Garter.

Actually, it is not the truth at all. Modern scholars tell us that Bishop George of Cappadocia was nothing whatever to do with our St George who – if he ever existed – probably met a martyr's death near Lydda in the late third century.

It's some years since we've had any limericks, and all the most recent crop – in the 1989 Cracker – were in French. Now for a few English ones. The first, Kingsley Amis once told me, dates from 1940, when we were daily expecting an airborne invasion. The German parachutists, we were informed – many of whom would be disguised for some reason as nuns – would all speak perfect, unaccented English; it was important, therefore, to devise some test by which they could be identified. The most ingenious was to recite to them the following verse. If they were English, they would be sure to smile; if German they would look blank.

A young engine-driver named Hunt
Once took out his engine to shunt,
   Saw a runaway truck,
   And by shouting out 'Duck!'
Saved the life of the fellow in front.

In fact I suspect that verse to be rather more recent, and to be the work of that limériciste extraordinaire, Robert Conquest. He was certainly responsible for:

Charlotte Brontë cried 'Wow, sister, what a man!
He laid me face down on the Ottoman;
   Now don't you and Emily
   Go telling the femily –
But he spanked me upon my bare bottom, Anne!'

and also for the splendid one on the late Arnold Toynbee, told me by John Gross:

It's no use, when talking to Toynbee,
To pay him back in his own coin, be-
   cause talking such piss
   Would come wholly amiss –
But how would a kick in the groin be?

Prof. Conquest tells me that this last was 'one of a couple allegedly written about each other by Arnold Toynbee and Bertrand Russell'. The Russell one ran:

Said the learned philosopher Russell
'One can come without moving a muscle,
   When sufficiently blotto
   Just watch Lady Otto-
line's bum as it bursts from her bustle.'

Of unknown authorship – at least to me – is:

> A Magdalen don of divinity
> Had a daughter who kept her virginity.
>   The fellows at Magdalen
>   Were obviously dagdalen –
> It could never have happened at Trinity.

But this one, on a slightly higher plane, I know to be by Fr. Ronnie Knox:

> Oh Lord, forasmuch as without Thee
> We are not enabled to doubt Thee,
>   Help us, by Thy grace,
>   To convince the whole race
> It knows nothing whatever about Thee.

If some King of the earth have so large an extent of dominion, in north and south, as that he hath winter and summer together in his dominions, so large an extent, east and west, as that he hath day and night together in his dominions, much more hath God mercy and judgement together: He brought light out of darkness, not out of a lesser light; He can bring thy summer out of winter, though thou have no spring: though in the ways of fortune and understanding, or conscience, thou have been benighted till now, wintered and frozen, clouded and eclipsed, damped and benumbed, smothered and stupefied till now, – now God comes to thee, not as in the dawning of the day, not as in the bud of the spring, but as the sun at noon to illustrate all shadows, as the sheaves in harvest to fill all penuries: all occasions shall invite His mercies, and all times are His seasons.

John Donne

I kicked off the 1996 Cracker by quoting, in good faith, the story about cannibalism by the – I now know – wholly fictitious Sir Bulwark Bloode. His creator, the distinguished historian of the Empire Lawrence James, has recently owned up; but, he writes:

. . . there were plenty of real Bloodes about in the nineteenth century, and I was encountering them through their volumes of reminiscences as part of my research for *The Rise and Fall of the British Empire*, which was published in 1994. Bluff, hearty fellows, they wrote in a no-nonsense manner about vigorous lives spent scrapping with assorted Mullahs and Malay pirates. Bloode himself was a hybrid, combining the qualities of the real Captain Sir Lambton Lorraine, who laid down the law in Spanish America in the 1870s, and General Sir George Younghusband, who spent much time doing the same thing in India in between grumbling about the deterioration of standards in officers' messes. His two volumes of memories are a rich quarry.

I have continued to trace imaginary adventures for Sir Bulwark. A dauntless midshipman in command of a pinnace cutting out a Russian clipper running vodka to Sebastopol, a stern commander forcing a Turkish pasha to holystone the decks of the ironclad *Cerberus* after an unpleasant incident with lady tourists in Beirut, and a grizzled admiral leading his bluejackets through the West African jungle to save some embattled resident. *Who's Who* for 1911 says it all:

BLOODE OF THE BIGHT, Admiral Lord (*cr.* 1890) **Bulwark Jervis Bloode**, CB 1885, Kt 1887; *b* 12 May 1840; 2nd *s* of late Rev. Pitt Bloode, Hereditary Archdeacon of West Meath; *m* 1875, Horatia, *d* of Admiral Sir Rodney Bevil; seven *s*. Midshipman HMS *Venomous* Sebastopol (medal & clasp); cmd. sloop HMS *Pug* Second China War (medal & 3 clasps, mentioned in despatches); captain cruiser HMS *Myrmidon*, Sydney station, 1860–67; captain HMS *Cerberus*, Mediterranean Fleet, served in Alexandria & Egyptian campaign, Sudan campaign (medal with 4 clasps); admiral commanding West Africa station, 1887–95, in cmd, of Mango River expedition 1889 and Calabar Field Force, 1890 (medal with 2 clasps & barony); commander, Mediterranean Fleet, 1869–97; retd. 1898. *Publications:* Lay on Hard: How Boxing Improves Stamina and Health of the Young Sailor, 1897; Notes on the Game Birds of Sierra Leone, 1898; Plain Words from an Old Salt: How Reform will Scupper the Fleet, 1904; A Warning from the Quarterdeck: Remarks on Naval Discipline, 1905; Get Aloft! How we must Train our Sailors, 1906;

Swinging the Lead: Yarns from the China Seas, 1906; With the Flag on the Seven Seas, 1907; The Cutlass: its History and Uses, 1909; A Sportsman's Guide to the Big Game of the Suakin District, with Notes on Native Guides, 1910. *Recreations:* Boxing, shooting, riding. *Address:* The Lashings, Crabton Hardtack, Hampshire. *Clubs:* United Services.

We have done with dogma and divinity,
      Easter and Whitsun past,
The long, long Sundays after Trinity
      Are with us at last,
The passionless Sundays after Trinity,
      Neither feast-day nor fast.

Christmas comes with plenty,
      Lent spreads out its pall,
But these are five and twenty,
      The longest Sundays of all;
The placid Sundays after Trinity,
      Wheat-harvest, fruit-harvest, fall.

Spring with its burst is over,
      Summer has had its day,
The scented grasses and clover
      Are cut, and dried into hay;
The singing birds are silent,
      And the swallows flown away.

Post pugnam pausa fiet;
      Lord, we have made our choice;
In the stillness of autumn quiet
      We have heard the still, small voice.
We have sung *Oh where shall Wisdom?*
      Thick paper, folio, Boyce.

Let it not all be sadness,
      Not *omnia vanitas,*
Stir up a little gladness
      To lighten the *Tibi cras;*
Send us that little summer
      That comes with Martinmas.

When still the cloudlet dapples
      The windless cobalt blue,
And the scent of gathered apples
      Fills all the store-rooms through.
The gossamer silvers the bramble,
      The lawns are gemmed with dew.

An end of tombstone Latinity,
      Stir up sober mirth,
Twenty-fifth after Trinity,
      Kneel with the listening earth,
Behind the Advent trumpets,
      They are singing Emmanuel's birth.

John Meade Falkner

Falkner, author of that wonderful novel The Nebuly Coat, *was – rather surprisingly – Chairman of Armstrong Whitworth, the armaments manufacturers – 'a position', sniffs the* Dictionary of National Biography, *'in which he could hardly be called a success'.*

Many years ago, Judy Gendel taught me the French translation of 'It's a long way to Tipperary':

> C'est à Tip, Tip, à Tipperary
> Où nous allons, mes amis,
> Et c'est chic, chic, à Tipperary
> Mais mon dieu, c'est loin d'ici –
> Où est ce Tipperary?
> J'm'en fous, et toi aussi,
> Mais c'est pour Tip, Tip, Tip, pour Tipperary
> Que nous quittons Paris!

Paddy Leigh Fermor has since given me the Hindustani version:

> Burra dur hai Tipperary,
> Burra dur hai jhani ko;
> Burra dur hai Tipperary,
> Mera chokri dekhne ko;
> Salaam, Piccadilly!
> Ram-ram, Leicester Square!
> Burra-burra dur hai Tipperary,
> Lekin mera dil hai waha.

How many other London place-names appear in verse or song? Eleven years ago I quoted Charles Johnston's 'Air Travel in Arabia':

> Then Petra flashed by in a wink;
> It looked like Eaton Square – but pink.

Nor should we forget that inspired verse from 'The Night I appeared as Macbeth', an old music-hall song by W. F. Hargreaves:

> I acted so tragic, the house rose like magic,
> The audience yelled 'You're sublime!'
> They made me a present of Mornington Crescent –
> They threw it a brick at a time.

How to compose operatic overtures: a letter from Gioacchino Rossini, giving advice to a young colleague:

Wait till the evening before the opening night. Nothing primes inspiration like necessity, whether it takes the form of a copyist waiting for your work or the coercion of an exasperated impresario tearing his hair out in handfuls. In my day all the impresarios in Italy were bald at thirty.

I wrote the overture to *Otello* in a little room at the Barbaja Palace, in which the baldest and fiercest of these impresarios had locked me by force with nothing but a plate of *maccheroni* and the threat that I should not leave the room alive until I had written the last note. I wrote the overture to *La Gazza Ladra* on the day of the first performance in the theatre itself, where I was imprisoned by the director and watched over by four stage-hands, who had instructions to throw my manuscript out of the window page by page to the copyists who were waiting to transcribe it below. In the absence of pages, they were to throw me.

With the *Barber* I did better still. I didn't compose an overture, but simply took one which had been meant for an *opera semiseria* called *Elisabetta*. The public was delighted.

The overture to *Conte Ory* I wrote while fishing, with my feet in the water, in the company of Signor Aguado who was talking about Spanish finance. The one for *William Tell* was done under more or less similar circumstances. As for *Mosè*, I just didn't write one at all.

For be it never so derke
Me thinketh I see him ever mo.

Chaucer

Bonus

Among the nineteenth-century figures I should most like to have met is Henry Peter Brougham, later the first Lord Brougham and Vaux. Charles Greville, in his diary for 2 January 1828, describes him thus:

> About three weeks ago I passed a few days at Panshanger, where I met Brougham; he came from Saturday till Monday morning, and from the hour of his arrival to that of his departure he never ceased talking . . . Brougham is certainly one of the most remarkable men I ever met; to say nothing of what he is in the world, his almost childish gaiety and animal spirits, his humour mixed with sarcasm, but not ill-natured, his wonderful information, and the facility with which he handles every subject, from the most grave and severe to the most trifling, displaying a mind full of varied and extensive information and a memory which has suffered nothing to escape it, I never saw any man whose conversation impressed me with such an idea of his superiority over all others. As Rogers said the morning of his departure, 'this morning Solon, Lycurgus, Demosthenes, Archimedes, Sir Isaac Newton, Lord Chesterfield and a great many more went away in one post chaise.'

On 22 November he adds:

> Be Brougham's political errors what they may, his gaiety, temper and admirable social qualities make him delightful, to say nothing of his more solid merits, of liberality, generosity and charity; for charity it is to have taken the whole family of one of his brothers who is dead – nine children – and maintained and educated them.
>
> But even Brougham had a rival, of whom he was deeply jealous: Macaulay. Stephen[1] said that, if ever Macaulay's life was written by a competent biographer it would appear that he had displayed feats of memory which he believed to be unequalled by any human being. He can repeat all Demosthenes by heart, and all Milton, a great part of the Bible, both in English and (the New Testament) in Greek; besides this his memory retains passages innumerable of every description of books, which in discussion he pours forth with incredible facility. He is

---

[1] James Stephen, 1789–1859, Under-Secretary of State for the Colonies.

passionately fond of Greek literature; has not much taste for Latin or French. Old Mill[2] (one of the best Greek scholars of the day), thinks Macaulay has a more extensive and accurate acquaintance with the Greek writers than any man living, and there is no Greek book of any note which he has not read over and over again. In the Bible he takes great delight, and there are few better Biblical scholars. In law he made no proficiency, and mathematics he abominates; but his great forte is history, especially English history. Here his superhuman memory, which appears to have the faculty of digesting and arranging as well as of retaining, has converted his mind into a mighty magazine of knowledge, from which, with the precision and correctness of a kind of intellectual machine, he pours forth stores of learning, information, precept, example, anecdote, and illustration with a familiarity and facility not less astonishing than delightful.

... Brougham, tall, thin, and commanding in figure, with a face which, however ugly, is full of expression, and a voice of great power, variety, and even melody, notwithstanding his occasional prolixity and tediousness, is an orator in every sense of the word. Macaulay, short, fat, and ungraceful, with a round, thick, unmeaning face, and with rather a lisp, though he has made speeches of great merit, and of a very high style of eloquence in point of composition, has no pretensions to be put in competition with Brougham in the House of Commons. Nor is the difference and the inferiority of Macaulay less marked in society. Macaulay, indeed, is a great talker, and pours forth floods of knowledge on all subjects; but the gracefulness, lightness, and variety are wanting in his talk which are so conspicuous in his writings; there is not enough of alloy in the metal of his conversation; it is too didactic, it is all too good, and not sufficiently flexible, plastic and diversified for general society. Brougham, on the other hand, is all life, spirit and gaiety – 'from grave to gay, from lively to severe' – dashing through every description of folly and fun, dealing in those rapid transitions by which the attention and imagination are arrested and excited; always amusing, always instructive, never tedious, elevated to the height of the greatest intellect, and familiar with the most abstruse subjects, and at the same moment conciliating the humble pretensions of inferior minds by dropping into the midst of their pursuits and objects with a fervour and intensity of interest which surprises and delights his associates, and, above all, which puts them at their ease.

Brougham became Lord Chancellor in 1830, but is probably better known nowadays

[2] Philosopher, father of John Stuart Mill.

for inventing the type of carriage that bears his name (described by the poet Thomas Moore as 'an old little sort of garden chair') and for his discovery of a small and insignificant village on the Mediterranean coast of France by the name of Cannes, where he built a house. The Côte d'Azur was thus largely his invention. He was an ardent Francophile: according to the Dictionary of National Biography, *'when the French provisional government of 1848 summoned the National Assembly, Brougham was seized with a desire to be returned as deputy, and applied to the Minister of Justice for a certificate of naturalization. After some difficulty he was made to understand that if he became a French citizen he would lose his English citizenship, and with it his rank, offices, and emoluments, and he accordingly withdrew his request.'*

While I was at it, I also looked up Macaulay, who seems to have hated Brougham almost as much as Brougham hated him. The article also stresses his astonishing memory – he used to maintain that 'any fool can say his Archbishops of Canterbury backwards'. Never in his life, so far as is known, did he have a love affair.

A
Christmas
Cracker

1998

When Joanna David and I did a poetry reading at Stratford last year, she produced this marvellous poem from the Greek Anthology. It is by the epigrammatist and poet Hedylus of Samos, writing in the third century BC. The translation is by Louis Untermeyer.

With wine, and words of love, and every vow
    He lulled me into bed and closed my eyes;
A sleepy, stupid innocent – so now
    I dedicate the spoils of my surprise.
The silk that bound my breasts, my virgin zone,
    The cherished purity I could not keep;
Goddess, remember: we were all alone,
    And he was strong – and I was half asleep.

It reminded me of that lovely remark of Sir John Harington – who lived from 1561 to 1612, and is better known for his invention of the water closet – which I quoted in a Cracker *just a quarter of a century ago:*

For that same sweet sin of lechery, I would say as the Friar said: A young man and a young woman in a green arbour on a May morning – if God do not forgive it, I would.

This house, which is a very ancient one, was the birthplace of Ann de Boleyne. Not much matter; for she married the King while his real wife was alive. She, no more than Cranmer, seems, in her last moment, to have remembered her sins against her lawful queen. Foxe's Book of Martyrs, that ought to have been called Book of Liars, says Cranmer, the recanter and re-recanter, held out his offending hand in the flames, and cried out, 'that hand, that hand!' If he had cried out 'Catherine! Catherine!' I should have thought better of him; but it is clear that the story is a lie, invented by protestants to whitewash the character of this perfidious hypocrite and double apostate who, if bigotry had something to do in bringing him to the stake, certainly deserved his fate.

So wrote William Cobbett, surely one of the great masters of invective in our literature. Here he is on another of our heroes, Samuel Johnson:

Old dread-death and dread-devil Johnson, that teacher of moping and melancholy. If the writings of this time-serving, mean, dastardly old pensioner had got a firm hold of the people at large, the people would have been bereft of their souls. These writings, aided by the charm of their pompous sound, were fast making their ways, till light, reason and the French Revolution confined them to the shelves of repentant, married old rakes and those of old stock-jobbers with young wives standing in need of something to keep down their unruly ebullitions.

And yet how beautifully and simply Cobbett can write of the natural world around him:

I like to look at the winding side of a great down, with two or three numerous flocks of sheep in it, belonging to different farms; and to see lower down, the folds in the fields ready to receive them for the night.

The early part of 1998 produced a particularly striking indication of the danger nowadays to persons in high positions of an excessively mouvementé *sex life. How much more sensible, one feels, was the attitude apparently prevailing in America some eighty years ago. When in 1919 the presidential candidate Warren Gamaliel Harding was campaigning for election and some heckler raised the question of his notoriously unrestrained libido, the agent would leap to his feet with the words:*

We're not running this horse as a gelding.

On one occasion Harding, when President, was obliged to hustle one of the ladies of his acquaintance – she happened also to be the mother of his child – into a closet while he received the British ambassador. (See Nan Britton, The President's Daughter, *New York 1927.)*

My commonplace book contains two quotations from Harding's own speeches. The first is:

Progress is not proclamation nor palaver. It is not pretence nor play on prejudice. It is not the perturbation of a people passion-wrought, nor a promise proposed.

The second is rather less high-flown:

I carry no bitterness in my heart which dates from 1912.

Of cord and cassia-wood is the lute compounded;
Within it lie ancient melodies.
Ancient melodies – weak and savourless,
Not appealing to present men's taste.
Light and colour are faded from the jade stops;
Dust has covered the rose-red strings.
Decay and ruin came to it long ago,
But the sound that is left is still cold and clear.
I do not refuse to play it, if you want me to;
But even if I play, people will not listen.

How did it come to be neglected so?
Because of the Ch'iang flute and the zithern of Ch'in.

Po Chu-I (722–846)
Tr. Arthur Waley

Our dear friend Arthur Waley was staying with us at Renishaw, and my father very much admired his translations of Chinese poetry . . . Upon a Sunday morning, then, my father was walking round the lake which he had caused to be created, regretting that he had not moved the old river-bed further back, and thinking out possible fantasies in stone, torrents to fall through the hanging woods above, pavilions upon islands and decorative effects generally (a few years before, he had determined to have all the white cows in the park stencilled with a blue Chinese pattern, but the animals were so obdurate and perverse as in the end to oblige him to abandon the scheme). The lake is shaped like an hour-glass or a figure-of-eight, and a bridge spans its waist. On this bridge my father met Arthur Waley advancing towards him. Each took his hat off ceremoniously and said to the other, 'How much I wish we were going in the same direction!' and passed on. Half an hour later they met again at the same place, having pursued their contrary courses as though they were planets whose goings and comings are immutably fixed by the sun, and repeated their salutation.

Osbert Sitwell,
Left Hand, Right Hand!

In April 1775 seven hundred British troops were despatched to Danbury, Connecticut, to destroy secret stockpiles of arms amassed by the local farmers. While there they took the opportunity to burn some forty houses, warehouses and barns. Soon, however, they found themselves outnumbered and were obliged to retreat towards the little town of Ridgefield. At the north end of the town American troops commanded by Benedict Arnold were awaiting them and a number of British soldiers were killed, though the majority escaped to boats on Long Island Sound. It was a very minor affair by military standards, but it was the first armed confrontation in the American War of Independence. An ancient cannonball can still be seen embedded in the wall of the old Keeler Tavern. Sunk into that of the cemetery there is a plaque reading:

In defense of American independence at the Battle of Ridgefield, April 27, 1775, died Eight Patriots who were laid in this ground, Companioned by Sixteen British Soldiers. Living, their enemies, Dying, their guests.

In the 1996 Cracker I quoted the quatrain composed jointly by André Gide, Pierre Louÿs and Paul Valéry:

Gloire aux barbes de fer nocturnement éparses,
Effarant leurs poils morts dans les bras étendus
Les sols, de corps jonchés au choc des métatarses
Ont vaporisé l'or des sables épandus.

and promised to print in the next number any satisfactory translations that might be submitted. Alas, I failed to do so, but here now are four, with apologies for the delay. The first comes from John Drummond:

Long life to iron whiskers black as soot,
Dead hair scared scarce by reaching arm and hand;
The earth, with bodies strewn, tramped underfoot,
Converts to steaming gold the scattered sand.

Michael Birkett sent in no less than three. The first, by Arthur S*mons:

How many nights have thinned this silver beard?
What coils been cast, amid th' encircling arms?
The earth, all heavy with your footfall's tread,
Has turned to dreams the lonely golden sands.

The second, by Ted Hug*es:

Dazzled with the night's shredding sits Ironbeard,
Ghastly hide flaking, the arms pincers,
Earth choking with heel-smashed corpses
    And Sahara nuked.

Finally the third, by A. E. Ho*sman:

The gleaming beard is shaven
    By every wandering star;
The soul of man sheds lightly
    The arms they stretch so far.

The soil is thick with echoes
    Of lads whose feet have trod
The golden sands of morning
    Which do not lead to God.

[*The above translations were the only ones I had room for in the* 1998 Cracker. *One of the advantages of the present bound volume is that it allows me to include two more. The first comes from Professor Jacques Heyman, formerly Professor of Engineering at Cambridge University. He points out that in the original 'the lines were written sequentially – that is, a line once written was immutable. Ideas and images could be carried forward, but no return was possible to tinker with previous lines. Thus the idea of scattering, for which three different words are used, does move through the quatrain, but only one way.' He therefore suggests the following:*

> All praise for razor wire deployed in smattered night
> Outstretched axillae vaunt their splattered sable hair
> Phalangal impacts blast the earth to shattered fright
> And golden sands dissolve in scattered midnight air.

The second comes from my friend Adam Fergusson, who writes: 'I thought for a space that these words were heavy with symbolism – but not at all. They are a celebration of a sensible environmental measure taken by the Mairie at Trouville. With a little poetic licence (but not so much as to earn an endorsement) they might run thus:

> Hail the entanglements laid out by night,
> Their bristling wires impaling outstretched hands:
> Body-strewn beaches, trampled from our sight,
> Have stol'n the burnish from the rolling sands.']

One of the most curious footnotes to history I know is that which concerns the fate of the heart of Louis XIV. I quote from a letter received a few years ago from my friend Quentin Crewe:

As I think I told you, while the bodies of the Kings of France were buried at the church of St Denis, the hearts used to go to a church in the Loiret. Anne of Austria, the wife of Louis XIII, instituted a new practice. She built Val de Grâce, and it became the new repository for royal hearts. (Incidentally, I believe she crawled from the Bishop's Palace in Apt to the Cathedral there, in order to pray before the bones of St Anne for a son.) Her heart, Charles I's wife's heart and, ultimately, Louis XIV's heart were put in silver cases in Val de Grâce. It was in the scrum outside the church during the Revolution that a member of the Harcourt family found himself holding the case with Louis XIV's heart in it.

In the Harcourt papers, there is an inventory of the contents of Nuneham Manor. It says that in the drawing room there is 'a small case which formerly contained a portion of the heart of Louis XIV, obtained at Val de Grâce when spoliation took place during the French Revolution'. The papers do not say what happened to the heart. They merely state that 'the case still remains, but the contents came to an extraordinary ending in 1848'. The family story was that Dr William Buckland, Dean of Westminster, who was also a mineralogist holding the Chair at Oxford, came to dinner. It was his boast that he could tell any mineral by its taste. The heart looked a little like a piece of pumice stone by this time; Buckland was blindfolded and given it as a joke to identify. He was so shocked by the taste of formaldehyde that he gasped, swallowed the heart by mistake, and – according to one version of the story – died the same night.

The last point is in fact inaccurate: Buckland lived on until 1856. The silver case – now of course empty – still lies on a chest in the dining room, beneath a portrait of Dr Buckland. There is also a contemporary poem entitled 'Conversation at Dinner, 1848'; the poem relates the story and ends with these lines:

> Here lies a Very Reverend shade,
>   A man of parts,
> Who holds, until the last trump's played,
>   The Ace of Hearts.

The Dictionary of National Biography *reports that:*

A brother geologist of eminence described Buckland as 'cheery, humorous, bustling, full of eloquence, with which he too blended much true wit; seldom without his famous blue bag, whence, even at fashionable evening parties, he would bring out and describe with infinite drollery, amid the surprise and laughter of his audience, the last "find" from a bone cave'. The following quotation is from a letter of Sir Roderick Murchison's, at the time of the meeting of the British Association at Bristol: 'At that meeting the fun of one of the evenings was a lecture of Buckland's. In that part of his discourse which treated of ichnolites, or fossil footprints, the Doctor exhibited himself as a cock or hen on the edge of a muddy pond, making impressions by lifting one leg after another. Many of the grave people thought our science was altered to buffoonery by an Oxford Don.'

Of all the wild absurdities
With which the heart can cram
Its sad asylum, none's more daft
Than this mad need, this damn
Idiot ache to be with you
When I already am.

Kiowara no Fokayabo, ninth century,
translated by Graeme Wilson

The death of John Wells on 11 January 1998 has been a sad loss to his countless friends and admirers. Here – slightly abridged for reasons of space – is his obituary of his mother-in-law. It appeared in The Times *on 29 October 1996.*

Sylvia Chancellor was one of the wittiest and most entertaining women of her generation. Till well into her nineties she delighted her sixteen grandchildren, hammering the piano and singing Edwardian music-hall songs like 'Now my mother-in-law is dead' (she got stuck in a folding bed which his friends want to borrow).

As a child, Sylvia once had to drive through Somerset in a pony-cart, begging food to feed her hungry brothers and sisters. This was not because of poverty but because of the wild irresponsibility of her parents. Her father, Sir Richard Paget, was not a practical provider. He spent his time at Oxford training his dog to say 'Lola, I love you' and attached wireless transmitters to seals in the First World War to send back information on German U-boats. At Cranmore he built a bird's nest and lived in it for several weeks. Her mother, Lady Muriel, was often in Eastern Europe, rescuing English governesses from revolution.

Sylvia assisted her father in his experiments – one involved quite a serious fall jumping off a fast-moving bus to prove that if you leaned forward you would land on your feet – and trailed round Canada with him demonstrating his artificial voice-box. He also taught her to hum one tune, whistle a harmony and tap a third out on her cheek, all at the same time. Soon after she graduated from Newnham she met her future husband Christopher. He joined Reuters, working his way up to become Far Eastern Manager, when they moved to Shanghai. There she dominated the English colony, directing a much-praised production of *The Beggar's Opera*. When the Japanese arrived in her garden she successfully ordered them off the grass. Later they arrested her on the Trans-Siberian Railway and put her in prison in Korea, where she demanded and got a daily copy of *The Times*. When brought to Tokyo to be told she was free she insisted on them paying her fare back to Shanghai.

In England, with her house full of evacuated children, her target practice with her husband's revolver terrified the neighbours, who said they would prefer a German invasion, and the house caught fire so often that she greeted the local brigade with a cry of 'Gentlemen, take your accustomed places!' Throughout the war she worked at the Czech Institute, and when their first-floor flat was bombed she continued to use it, climbing a ladder through the gutted ground floor beneath.

She drilled her children to sing part-songs for a wide variety of guests, including the Emperor of Japan, Clement Attlee and Kwame Nkrumah. Her most serious achievement was founding the Prisoners' Wives

Service, after seeing the distress of her cleaner in London whose husband had been arrested at four in the morning. With inspired energy and irresistibly charming bossiness she enlisted the help of Roy Jenkins and Lord Louis Mountbatten, and was awarded the OBE.

She continued to be dazzling and eccentric. She began renovating the Priory at Ditcheat when she and her husband were approaching eighty, entirely redecorating it and making a new garden. 'When we get *really* geriatric,' she said, 'we're going to live in New York.' Her last days were in fact spent, very happily, in a little cottage in Shellingford, where she continued to entertain and delight everyone in the village.

*Major R. B. Kennard of Lambourn – introducing himself as 'an old Qu'hai' –
was much struck by the Hindustani version of 'Tipperary' in last year's Cracker
– so much, indeed, that he very kindly sent me another translation into the same
language. It runs as follows:*

> Jehaz par ek larki boli:
> 'Kitne dárd hai jab peshád karti.'
>   'Ah-ha', bola murd,
>   'Mujh-ko bhi aisa dárd
> Aur captain aur dafadar bhi.'

*The English version – which at the time I had not heard before, but which I have
since found, only slightly disguised, in Norman Douglas's wonderfully filthy
collection – goes like this:*

> There was a young lady at sea
> Who said 'My, how it hurts when I pee.'
>   'Ah-ha', said the mate,
>   'That accounts for the state
> Of the captain, the bo'sun and me.'

An introduction to a set of remarkably poor postcards depicting the Canal du Midi at different seasons of the year:

The 'Canal du Midi' is musical. He gently sings when he flows through some villages with cheerful names. He swanks in Toulouse, seems cheerless in Carcassonne and dresses with plenty of sluice-gates in Béziers. As soon as he leaves the city and approaches Capestang, Argeliers, Le Rodorte, Homps Puicherie, Marseillette, he lets his good temper out. Careless in the heart of the countries changing at the mercy of seasons and flower-time, he heems the gay melody of those who have time. Calm river arm here, swan dock there, he farther becomes a timeless harbour or the monumental lane of a forgotten park, every curve reveals a surprise repeated at every period of the year. You, who are listening to his quiet purl, don't beware these still waters for they carry the traveller's dream.

Ninety-nine years to the day before my own birth, Mr William Huskisson MP attended the opening of the Manchester–Liverpool Railway and was unfortunately run over by the locomotive. The scene of the tragedy – on the line near Newton-le-Willows – is marked by a memorial of vaguely Soanian design, bearing the following inscription:

THIS TABLE
A tribute of personal respect and affection
has been placed here to mark the spot where on the
15th of September 1830 the day of the opening of this rail road
THE RIGHT HONble WILLIAM HUSKISSON MP
singled out by the decree of an inscrutable providence from
the midst of the distinguished multitude that surrounded him
in the full pride of his talents and the perfection of his
usefulness met with the accident that occasioned his death
which deprived England of an illustrious statesman
and Liverpool of its most honoured representative which changed
a moment of the noblest exaltation and triumph that science and
genius had ever achieved into one of desolation and mourning
and striking terror into the hearts of assembled thousands
brought home to every bosom the forgotten truth that
IN THE MIDST OF LIFE WE ARE IN DEATH

Could this, I wonder, be the longest single sentence ever carved in stone? It reminds me of those somewhat pithier lines by – surprisingly enough – A. E. Housman, first quoted to me by Duff Hart-Davis:

'Hallelujah!' was the only observation
That escaped Lieutenant-Colonel Mary Jane,
When she tumbled off the platform in the station
And was cut in little pieces by the train.
        Mary Jane, the train is through yer;
        Hallelujah, Hallelujah!
We will gather up the fragments that remain.

'Fragments' is, I think, the operative word.

It is necessary for technical reasons that these warheads be stored upside down; that is, with the top at the bottom and the bottom at the top. In order that there may be no doubt as to which is the bottom and which is the top, it will be seen to that the bottom of each warhead immediately be labelled with the word TOP.

British Admiralty Regulation,
quoted in *Applied Optics*, vii, 19 (1968)

Tony Quinton long ago called my attention to the following extract from a sermon preached by Dr Edward Pusey on 1 March 1861 in St Mary's church, Oxford, to 'the Younger Members of the University'. The sermon was entitled 'The Thought of the Love of Jesus for us, the Remedy for Sins of the Body'. The extract is quoted in The Life of Oscar Browning *by Ian Anstruther.*

But in the trial itself, especially in that sort which (those whom it concerns will know what I mean) comes when no one is by . . . I know but one effectual remedy – to clasp the hands together, and pray earnestly to God for help . . . Fearful and common those punishments are, which I have seen and known and read of. I have known of manifold early death; I have seen the fineness of intellect injured; powers of reasoning, memory impaired; nay, insanity, oftentime idiotcy [sic]; every form of decay of mind and body; consumption too often, torturing death, even of a strong frame. Lesser degrees of those punishments were God's warning voice: at first bodily growth checked, eyesight perhaps distressed or impaired; that fine, beautiful, delicate system which carries sensation through the whole human frame, in whatever degree, harmed, and for the most part, in that degree irreparably. When these warnings were neglected further decay, with scarce an exception, visibly followed.

Dr Pusey forgot, unfortunately, two other well-known symptoms of addiction to solitary vice. First, there is the 'long, thin, almost imperceptible black hair growing out of the palm of the left hand' (see More Christmas Crackers, *p. 316). Second, your ears fall off.*

It is a great nuisance getting old and never knowing whether you haven't said 'Jerusalem' when you meant 'Paddington'.

Gilbert Murray

De mon château jusqu'à Venise
Mon chien est mort, puis mon cheval.
Les voleurs ne m'ont pas fait mal:
J'ai pu garder la route prise.

De Venise à l'Ile de Malte
Mes cinq amis ont chu en mer . . .
Il me restait l'épée de fer
A Saint-Jean d'Acre pour la halte.

Entre Saint-Jean de Terre Sainte
Et les murs de Jérusalem
Mon âme a fui dans un harem
Avec mon coeur, sans une plainte.

Je n'ai plus d'or, de chien, de selle.
– Oh! compagnons, priez pour moi!
Car l'amour tue comme la croix . . .
Je n'ai que toi, mon Infidèle!

Diane Lyves

This pretty little poem was sent me by my friend Professor Sir Alan Harris, who knows almost as much about France and her literature as he knows about pre-stressed concrete – which is a very great deal. Of its author I have discovered only that in 1980 she won the Prix Poésie Richard de Bas, awarded her by the Musée de Poésie at Carpentras. How nice to have a Museum of Poetry; does anywhere else, I wonder?

Late August, given heavy rain and sun
For a full week, the blackberries would ripen.
At first, just one, a glossy purple clot
Among others, red, green, hard as a knot.
You ate that first one and its flesh was sweet
Like thickened wine; summer's blood was in it
Leaving stains upon the tongue and lust for
Picking. Then red ones inked up and that hunger
Sent us out with milk-cans, pea-tins, jam-pots,
Where briars scratched and wet grass bleached our boots.
Round hayfields, cornfields and potato-drills
We trekked and picked until the cans were full,
Until the tinkling bottom had been covered
With green ones, and on top big dark blobs burned
Like a plate of eyes. Our hands were peppered
With thorn pricks, our palms sticky as Bluebeard's.

We hoarded the fresh berries in the byre.
But when the bath was filled we found a fur,
A rat-grey fungus, glutting on our cache.
The juice was stinking too. Once off the bush
The fruit fermented, the sweet flesh would turn sour.
I always felt like crying. It wasn't fair
That all the lovely canfuls smelt of rot.
Each year I hoped they'd keep, knew they would not.

Seamus Heaney

ON HIS BLACKBERRIES GONE MOULDY
FOR SEAMUS HEANEY

You should have put them down to turn to wine
to yeast with sugar, bubble for a month
then strain and syphon off in casks
let them lie still while a twelvemonth turns
watching them to see no wild yeasts bloom
their sweet to sour, no vinegar fly
lays bitter droppings in their bloody depths.

Come the next year you could have run them off
last August caught, the sun and dark spiced fruit
the bramble gift, gratuitous, casual as sudden love
have lit another year, mellowed next winter's frost
with native Falernian, in heady classical
tradition of friendship and fireside;
instead you let the mildew have them.

Not your fault of course; what you were brought up to
since the fall of limbs from that Judas tree
a rigor mortis that cramps us still
in crucifixion postures to blight
even the innocent berries on the hill
as if our hands were leprous from playing
with ourselves in lieu of others. You let despair
dictate their decay. Fruits can rise up in wine
love in the linked flesh, transmute by a barm of lust
sugared with words and gestures, laid by
in absence to drink and drink again
in the warm bed of winter
lightening our darkness, a gentle lunacy
we sip and sip to keep us sane.

Lost vintage of blackberries you squandered
preach sermons for me. Time enough
for a shroud of mould when the sun goes down
in our eyes. These autumn hills
are clothed with bracken for beds, ripe with
heavy fall fruits I can grow drunk on; overnight
mushrooms mark where we lay. Behind nettles
and the slung silver of dewed webs hang
the reached treasures I crush into words
that may light equinox tapers in later eyes.

You have to have faith in fruits, top and tail
pick, turn over, add your fermenting heat to theirs
cosset the chemical change that will power
a rocket at the sun so that drawing the cork
long after connoisseurs may take
pleasure in this limbec, the bouquet
of mingled sweat, regather
the clove and cinnamon light of our hillside
where pleasures grow for the taking.

Maureen Duffy

[When I prepared the 1998 Cracker, these were the only two poems I knew about blackberries. Since then, however, a great friend – and the terrible thing is that I can't remember who (Hello Dr Alzheimer, I've heard so much about you) – has called my attention to a third. It is a villanelle by Mary Sheepshanks, and it is called 'The Bramble Route'.

I got beguiled by frozen blackberries:
they shone so lusciously from plastic trays;
no ripped up clothes, no bleeding hearts or knees.

The flavour's bland: why fall for charms like these
yet ache for sharper taste and wilder ways?
I got beguiled by frozen blackberries.

This cultivated fruit in my deep freeze
took me to superstores, by motorways –
no laddered tights, no bleeding heart or knees.

There cash-tills rang – not oreads in trees
to sing me madrigals of mountain days.
I got beguiled by frozen blackberries!

Synthetic sweetness, neatly-packaged ease,
sang blandishments from marketing displays:
'guaranteed not to scratch the heart or knees'.

Next time: a bramble route through scrub and screes,
a daring scramble – love's uncharted maze –
and I'll resist the frozen blackberries
to take a risk with clothes and heart and knees.

A wonderful passage by Jeremy Taylor:

For so have I seen a lark rising from his bed of grass, and soaring upwards, singing as he rises, and hopes to get to heaven, and climb above the clouds; but the poor bird was beaten back with the loud sighings of an eastern wind, and his motion made irregular and unconstant, descending more at every breath of the tempest than it could recover by the liberation and frequent weighing of his wings; till the little creature was forced to sit down and pant, and stay till the storm was over; and then it made a prosperous flight, and did rise and sing, as if it had learned music and motion from an angel as he passed sometimes through the air about his ministries here below.

And another:

However it be very easy to have our thoughts wander, yet it is our indifferency and lukewarmness that makes it so natural: and you may observe it, that so long as the light shines bright, and the fires of devotion and desires flame out, so long the mind of man stands close to the altar and waits upon the sacrifice; but as the fires die, and desires decay, so the mind steals away, and walks abroad to see the little images of beauty and pleasure, which it beholds in the falling stars and little glow-worms of the world.

What is the greatest understatement in history? I think I would award the palm to Arthur Balfour, our Prime Minister from 1902 to 1905. He also served as Foreign Secretary under Lloyd George from 1916 to 1919, in which capacity he signed the so-called Balfour Declaration of 1917, promising a national home in Palestine for the Jews. He remarked as he did so:

I have no idea what the result will be, but I am certain that it will lead to a very interesting situation.

Mochua and Columcille lived at the same time and Mochua, being a hermit in the waste, had no wordly goods but only a cock, a mouse and a fly. And the office of the cock was to keep the hour of matins for him. As for the mouse, it would never suffer him to sleep but five hours, day and night, and if he was like to sleep longer, being weary with vigils and prostrations, the mouse would fall to licking his ear till it woke him. And the fly's office was to be walking along each line of his psalter as he read it, and when he was weary with singing his psalms, the fly would abide upon the line where he left off until he could return again to the saying of the psalms. Now it came to pass that these three precious ones died soon. And upon that Mochua wrote a letter to Columcille in Alba, sorrowing for the death of his flock. Columcille replied to him, and this is what he said: 'My brother,' he said, 'marvel not that thy flock should have died, for misfortune ever waits upon wealth.'

O. J. Bergin,
Stories from Keating's History of Ireland

Two thumbnail sketches by Violet Trefusis, published in Horizon, November *1943. The first, on England:*

The land of pickles and tinned vegetables, draughts and rattling windows, 'dirty cads' and 'jolly good sorts'; hundred percent he-men and hundred percent he-women; of snubs and snobs, of smuts and guts; of area railings and window-boxes, of corns and 'dentures', of intrepid old maids and blushing giants; the land of placid parks and aspiring suburbs, of ghosts and curses, of drunkards and ascetics, of magnanimity and promiscuity, of beautiful children and witches, gentleness and depravity, innocence and trust, of business acumen and poetry, of gallantry and modesty, of honesty and prejudice, practical jokes and horseplay, puns and nicknames, gentility and class consciousness; the land of birds and flowers, fields and hedges, sport and loyalty, teas and breakfasts, inarticulateness and repression, whimsy and puerility, tradition and pageantry; the land whose national anthem is 'For he's a jolly good fellow', where it matters *how* you eat rather than *what* you eat, where your accent is more important than your vocabulary, where octogenarians are automatically canonized, where advertisements represent either toothless grandparents or their toothless grandchildren, where you may neglect your wife but not your dog, where you may be eccentric but not original, where you must be loyal to a friend rather than faithful to a woman. The land of hospitality and no manners, of hot baths and cold comfort, where the place in the heart matters more than the place at table. The land for men and children, dogs and flowers.

The second, on France:

The land of accelerated voices, faces, minds. The land of vituperation and irascibility, of malice and criticism, of wit and satire, of mothers-in-law and *tantes à héritage*, the land of *dots* and law-suits, *enterrement de première classe* and *lettres de faire-part*; the land of planes and poplars, of light and symmetry, of style and synthesis; the land of coffee and croissants, wood strawberries and a hundred cheeses, the land of black tobacco and matches which never strike; the land of derailed trains and devilish taxis; of perennial black (especially for travelling), hairy warts and tumours, stuffiness and *tisanes*, the land of ingenuity and improvisation, the land of waxed parquets and stilted furniture, form and formality, taste and tact, xenophobia and vindictiveness; the land of hideous gardens and beautiful perspectives, fountains and statues, discipline and economy, conversation and eloquence. The land of matriarchs and mistresses, family feuds and *bas de laine*, technique and tactics, sense and sensibility, impetus and panache. The land of ruthlessness and caprice, elegance and epicureanism, the land where people are urban rather than bucolic, gregarious rather than friendly, where they prefer form to colour, *chic* to beauty, revolution to change; the land where you may joke about almost anything except your mother and, still less, your grandmother, where excess seldom spells success, where culture, the family, decorum, protocol, prosperity are accorded the maximum respect; the land where it is most enjoyable to be (a) a woman, (b) an artist, (c) a cook, (d) a politician, (e) a dressmaker; where it is least enjoyable to be (1) an old maid, (2) a recluse, (3) a fool, (4) a *jeune fille*.

Forgive, O Lord, my little jokes on Thee,
And I'll forgive Thy great big one on me.

Robert Frost

Bonus

The things about you I appreciate
  May seem indelicate.
I'd like to find you in the shower
And chase the soap for half an hour.
I'd like to have you in my power
  And see your eyes dilate.
I'd like to have your back to scour
And other parts to lubricate.
Sometimes I feel it is my fate
To chase you screaming up a tower
  Or make you cower
By asking you to differentiate
  Nietzsche from Schopenhauer.
I'd like successfully to guess your weight
I'd like to offer you a flower.

I like the hair upon your shoulders
Falling like water over boulders.
I like the shoulders too; they are essential.
Your collar-bones have great potential.
(I'd like all your particulars in folders
  Marked *Confidential*.)

I like your cheeks, I like your nose,
I like the way your lips disclose
The neat arrangement of your teeth
(Half above and half beneath)
  In rows.
I like your eyes, I like their fringes.
The way they focus on me gives me twinges.
Your upper arms drive me berserk.
I like the way your elbows work
  On hinges.
I like your wrists, I like your glands,
I like the fingers on your hands.

I'd like to teach them how to count,
And certain things we might exchange,
Something familiar for something strange.
I'd like to give you just the right amount
    And get some change.

I like it when you tilt your cheek up.
I like the way you nod and hold a tea-cup.
I like your legs when you unwind them.
Even in trousers I don't mind them.
I like each softly moulded knee-cap.
I like the little crease behind them.
I'd always know, without a recap,
    Where to find them.

I like the sculpture of your ears.
I like the way your profile disappears
Whenever you decide to turn and face me.
I'd like to cross two hemispheres
    And have you chase me.
I'd like to smuggle you across frontiers,
Or sail with you at night into Tangiers.
    I'd like you to embrace me.

I'd like to see you ironing your shirt
    And cancelling other dates.
I'd like to button up your shirt.
I like the way your chest inflates.
I'd like to smoothe you when you're hurt,
Or frightened senseless by invert-
    ebrates.

I'd like you even if you were malign
And had a yen for sudden homicide.
I'd let you put insecticide
    Into my wine.
I'd even like you if you were the bride
    Of Frankenstein
Or something ghoulish out of Mamoulian's
    Jekyll and Hyde.
I'd even like you as my Julian
Of Norwich or Cathleen ni Houlihan.
    How melodramatic
If you were something muttering in an attic

Like Mrs Rochester or a student of Boolean
    Mathematics.

You are the end of self-abuse.
You are the eternal feminine.
I'd like to find a good excuse
To call on you and find you in.
I'd like to put my hand beneath your chin
    And see you grin.
I'd like to taste your Charlotte Russe;
I'd like to feel my lips upon your skin.
I'd like to make you reproduce.

I'd like you in my confidence.
I'd like to be your second look.
I'd like to let you try the French Defence
    And mate you with my rook.
I'd like to be your preference
    And hence
I'd like to be around when you unhook.
I'd like to be the only audience,
The final name in your appointment book,
    Your future tense.

John Fuller

A
Christmas
Cracker

1999

I found a few months ago, in Peter Vansittart's superb book In Memory of England, *the following words of Queen Victoria:*

These are trying moments, and it seems to me a defect in our much-famed constitution to have to part with an admirable govt: like Lord Salisbury's for no question of any importance, or any particular reason, merely on account of the number of votes.

In last year's Cracker we heard about Dr William Buckland, Professor of Geology at Oxford and consumer – inter alia – of the heart of Louis XIV. Bevis Hillier has recently sent me this memoir by the Rev. W. Tuckwell MA, in his Reminiscences of Oxford, *London 1901:*

I recall much earlier days, when I was wont to play with Frank Buckland and his brother in their home at the corner of Tom Quad: the entrance hall with its grinning monsters on the low staircase, of whose latent capacity to arise and fall upon me I never quite overcame my doubts; the side-table in the dining-room covered with fossils, 'PAWS OFF' in large letters on a protecting card; the very sideboard candlesticks perched on saurian vertebrae: the queer dishes garnishing the dinner-table – horseflesh, I remember more than once, crocodile another day, mice baked in batter on a third – while the guinea-pig under the table inquiringly nibbled at your infantine toes, the bear walked round your chair and rasped your hand with file-like tongue, the jackal's fiendish yell close by came through the open window, the monkey's hairy arm extended itself suddenly over your shoulder to annex your fruit and walnuts.

I think the Doctor rather scared us; we did not understand his sharp, quick voice and peremptory manner, and preferred the company of his kind, charming, highly cultured wife. Others found him alarming; dishonesty and quackery of all kinds fled from that keen, all-knowing vision. When Tom Tower was being repaired, he watched the workmen from his window with a telescope, and frightened a scamping mason whom he encountered descending from the scaffold by bidding him go back and bring down that faulty piece of work he had just put into a turret.

At Palermo, on his wedding tour he visited St Rosalia's shrine . . . It was opened by the priests, and the relics of the saint were shown. He saw that they were not Rosalia's: 'They are the bones of a goat,' he cried out, 'not of a woman'; and the sanctuary doors were abruptly closed. Frank used to tell of their visit long afterwards to a foreign cathedral where was exhibited a martyr's blood – dark spots on the pavement, ever fresh and ineradicable. The professor dropped on the pavement and touched the stain with his tongue. 'I can tell you what it is; it's bat's urine!'

Another recollection, by one G. C. Bompas, is cited in Christopher Hibbert's Encyclopaedia of Oxford:

Guinea-pigs were often running over the tables; and occasionally the pony, having trotted down the steps from the garden, would push open the dining-room door and career round the table, with three laughing children on his back . . . I was in chapel one Sunday when an eagle came in at the eight o'clock service . . . and advanced with its wings nearly spread out. Two or three people left their places to deal with it; Dean Gaisford looked unspeakable things . . . [Frank] told me one day what he had had for dinner the day before – namely panther chops! The panther had been buried for a couple of days. 'But,' said Buckland, 'I got them to dig it up and send me some. It was not very *good*.'

Apart from the unfortunate incident involving Louis XIV's heart, it is not clear whether Dr Buckland ever tried cannibalism – though I strongly suspect he did. I wonder what he would have made of the following little story, told by Vladimir Nabokov. It is included in his Poems and Problems, *and was first published in 1942 in the* New Yorker.

A LITERARY DINNER

Come here, said my hostess, her face making room
for one of those pink introductory smiles
that link, like a valley of fruit trees in bloom,
the slopes of two names.
I want you, she murmured, to eat Dr James.

I was hungry. The doctor looked good. He had read
the great book of the week and had liked it, he said,
because it was powerful. So I was brought
a generous helping. His mauve-bosomed wife
kept showing me, very politely I thought,
the tenderest bits with the point of her knife.
I ate – and in Egypt the sunsets are swell;
The Russians were doing remarkably well;
Had I met Prince Poprinsky, whom he had known
in Caporabella, or was it Mentone?
They had travelled extensively, he and his wife;
His hobby was People, her hobby was Life.
All was good and well-cooked, but the tastiest part
was his nut-flavoured, crisp cerebellum. The heart
resembled a shiny-brown date,
and I stowed all the studs on the edge of my plate.

The question of Sunday observance has always caused problems among the English – among the Scots, still more so. Things have loosened up a good deal in the past ten years, but in Hansard of 1 November 1988 it is interesting to find a speech by Earl Ferrers – who was then Minister of State at the Home Office – in which he says:

It is not for me to interpret the law. However, I did a little homework to find out the position on Sunday trading. As I understand it, one can sell on Sunday a pornographic magazine but not a Bible, unless the Bible happens to be sold at a designated airport or at a railway station. One can sell fried fish and chips at a restaurant but not at a fish and chip shop, where however one can sell any meal apart from fried fish and chips. One can sell tinned or untinned clotted cream and untinned unclotted cream, but not tinned unclotted cream.

Jan Morris has sent me this extract from the funeral service of the Emperor Franz Josef in 1916, pronounced at the entrance to the imperial burial vault – the Kaisergruft – beneath the Kapuzinerkirche in Vienna.

THE FATHER SUPERIOR: Who art thou? Who asks to be admitted here?

THE GREAT CHAMBERLAIN: I am His Majesty the Emperor of Austria, King of Hungary.

THE FATHER SUPERIOR: I know him not. Who asks to be admitted here?

THE GREAT CHAMBERLAIN: I am the Emperor Franz Josef, Apostolic King of Hungary, King of Bohemia, King of Jerusalem, Prince of Transylvania, Grand Duke of Tuscany and Cracow, Duke of Lorraine.

THE FATHER SUPERIOR: I know him not. Who asks to be admitted here?

THE GREAT CHAMBERLAIN: I am Franz Josef, a poor sinner, and I implore the mercy of God.

THE FATHER SUPERIOR: Then thou mayest enter.

[In the Cracker I located the ceremony in St Stephen's Cathedral; I was wrong, and am most grateful to those readers who put me right.]

Two passages about death – very different, but both quite cheerful in their respective ways. The first comes from Swinburne's A Forsaken Garden. *I'm not quite sure what it means, but it sounds marvellous:*

> Till the slow sea rise and the sheer cliff crumble,
> Till terrace and meadow the deep gulfs drink,
> Till the strength of the waves of the high tides humble
> The fields that lessen, the rocks that shrink;
> Here now, in his triumph, where all things falter,
> Stretched out on the spoils that his own hand spread,
> Like a god self-slain on his own strange altar,
>   Death lies dead.

The second – by contrast – is good, straight, sound common sense. But then, coming as it does from the pen of Montaigne, what else could it be?

Il faut penser à la mort. La nature nous y force. Sortez, dit-elle, de ce monde comme vous y êtes entré. Le même passage que vous fîtes de la mort à la vie, sans passion et sans frayeur, refaites-le de la vie à la mort. Si vous avez vécu un jour, vous avez tout vu. Il n'y a point d'autre lumière ni d'autre nuit. Si vous avez fait votre profit de la vie, vous en êtes repu. Faites place aux autres comme d'autres vous l'ont faite. Allez-vous-en satisfait.

We have to think of death. Nature obliges us to do so. Leave this world, she says, as you entered it. That same passage that you made from death to life, without passion and without fear, make again from life and death. If you have lived for a day, you have seen everything. There is no other light, no other darkness. If you have drawn any profit from your life, you have had enough of it. Make way for others, just as others made way for you. Go on your way satisfied.

And now here are two about wine. The first is by my father, Duff Cooper, and is taken from his autobiography, Old Men Forget:

Writing in my sixty-fourth year, I can truthfully say that since I reached the age of discretion I have consistently drunk more than most people would say was good for me. Nor do I regret it. Wine has been to me a firm friend and a wise counsellor. Often . . . wine has shown me matters in their true perspective and has, as though by the touch of a magic wand, reduced great disasters to small inconveniences. Wine has lit up for me the pages of literature, and revealed in life romance lurking in the commonplace. Wine has made me bold but not foolish; has induced me to say silly things but not to do them. Under its influence words have often come too easily which had better not have been spoken, and letters have been written which had better not have been sent. But if such small indiscretions standing in the debit column of wine's account were added up, they would amount to nothing in comparison with the vast accumulation on the credit side.

The second is by the great George Saintsbury:

There is no money, of the expenditure of which I am less ashamed, or which has given me better value.in return, than the price of the liquids chronicled in *Notes on a Cellar-Book.* When they were good they pleased my senses, cheered my spirits, improved my moral and intellectual powers, besides enabling me to confer the same benefits on other people. And whether they were bad or good, the grapes that had yielded them were the fruits of that Tree of Knowledge which, as the theologians too commonly forget to expound, it became not merely lawful but incumbent on us to use, with discernment, when our First Mother had paid the price for it, and handed it on to us to pay for likewise.

It is hard to conceive of two English writers more different from one another than Sir Philip Sidney and P. G. Wodehouse. My old friend Nathalie Brooke has however sent me a photograph of a plaque, attached to a medieval-looking brick tower in the city of Zutphen, which reads as follows:

To the Memory of
Sir Philip Sidney (1554–1586)
whose act of unselfish sacrifice
when wounded during the siege of Zutphen
became a substantial inspiration for
his fellow-author and compatriot

Sir Pelham G. Wodehouse (1881–1975)
20th century's foremost humorous author,
who has adorned several of his novels
with a farcical and rollicking
paraphrase of the incident.

sponsored by
Future Trend   P. G. Wodehouse Society

For several years, Kerry and Charlotte St Johnston produced an annual selection of the more intriguing items in the catalogues of their local sale rooms. In 1991 the list ran as follows:

An old Oriental runner
Coloured engraving after Dendy Sadler, 'Same to you dear'
Oxo cube tin, bust of Dickens and a giroscope [*sic*]
Two erns on plintles
Two half lizards
Watercolour, 'Chickens on the Track', Signed Mogadone
Two Faggeroyes
Postcard of the Lady Ratclif and another of pigs
Spelter figure of a wild boor being a pen wipe
Dior crocodile handbag and an old Fry chocolate box
Glazed pottery bear shaker and a leather parrot
Hair curlers, 4 bundles curtains and a stuffed bat
Pair of riding boots, folding camp bed and four chamber pots, one with
      grebe
A complete stuffed baby alligator with original hat
An oleograph study of a dying cow
A single volume, 'Dogs and their Doings', by the Rev. F. O. Morris
Watercolour of a hole, signed A. Shagyard, 1896

And in 1992:

Pair of miniature spaniards and a box of leather sundries
3 piece suit in Mustard and Green Dralon
Pair of Eastern Rubbings and a bedpan
A Belfast fink etc.
Three elaborately worked evening hags
Scotsman's brass knocker
A quantity of bunting and an Algerian fag
Six old flutes and a toffee hammer
Watercolour, 'Girl with Tits', B. Grummond, 1902
Cast Iron Gamekeeper
Oil, 'Sailors attempting to hook a boy', signed M. R. Flail
Print of a nude and the Mayor of Bristol
Engraved print of the Pruke of Northumberland
Stipple engraving, Lady and her little wog
An old pocket wizard

Print of deaf and dumb tramps
A french vaseline fish
The works of Josephus and a Pirelli calendar
An old hospital bed and a stuffed ferret
A box of bus terminators

A correspondence in The Times *in May 1991 on sedative sermons produced one memorable quotation. Mr J. F. Priestley told of a chaplain at Winchester whose opening words to the 'new men' on their first Sunday – all of them twelve-year-olds – were:*

Few of us can deny ourselves the intellectual pleasure of speculating upon the precise nature of the Pentecostal Gift . . .

A SONNET OF LINCOLN'S INN

Eros is ill at ease in Lincoln's Inn,
Where black-gowned justice has his sober rule,
And no one plays the hero or the fool;
But such as I sit, staid and bald, within,
Adding provisos to a saving clause,
Taming adventurous pleadings with red ink,
Gelding too bullish statements with 'I think',
Making the cause in hand my only cause.

Yet may he seek revenge one summer eve
And lead a rout of satyrs through New Square,
To chase – a thing no Bencher would believe –
Young naked girls with vine leaves in their hair,
And treat the startled judges with derision,
And make work for the family division.

Michael Albery, Q C

Many years ago – in 1965 to be precise – Harold Macmillan presented the Duff Cooper Prize to Professor Ivan Morris, for his book The World of the Shining Prince: A Description of Court Life in Tenth-Century Japan. *I think this extract gives the flavour:*

There were many occasions in daily life – a visit to the country, for example, or the sight of the first snowfall of the year – when failure to compose appropriate poems was a grave social solecism. Also, when one received a poem (on these or any other occasions) it was mandatory to send a prompt reply, preferably using the same imagery. As a rule, the ladies and gentlemen of Heian rose to the challenge. But there were times, we note almost with relief, when even these indefatigable versifiers faltered. The following passage from *The Pillow Book* (whose author, of course, was among the glibbest poets of her day) describes the return of the Empress Sakado's ladies from a cuckoo-viewing expedition, and provides one of those rare deviations from poetic etiquette.

'Well now,' said Her Majesty, 'where are they – where are your poems?'

We explained that we had not written any.

'Really?' she said. 'This is most unfortunate. The gentlemen at court will certainly have heard of your expedition. How are you going to explain that you do not have a single interesting poem to show for it? You should have jotted down something on the spur of the moment while you were listening to the cuckoos. But you wanted to make too much of the occasion and as a result you let your inspiration vanish. But you can still make up for it. Write something now!'

Everything Her Majesty said was true, and we were really distressed at our failure. I was discussing possible poems with the other ladies when a message arrived from the Fujiwara gentleman-in-waiting. His poem was attached to some white blossom and the paper itself was as white as the flower:

> *If only I had known*
> *That you were off to hear the cuckoo's song*
> *I should have sent my heart to join you on your way.*

Since the messenger was no doubt awaiting our reply, I asked someone to fetch an inkstone from our apartments, but the Empress ordered me to use hers. 'Write something at once,' she said. A piece of paper had been placed in the lid. 'Why don't you write the reply?'

I said to Lady Saisho. 'No, I'd rather you did it,' she answered.

'I still see no reason,' said Her Majesty, who was becoming angry, 'why those of you who went to hear the cuckoos can't write a proper poem about it. You seem to have set your minds against it.'

'But Your Majesty,' I said, 'by now the whole thing has become a bit dreary.'

There was no more talk about writing a poem for this particular occasion.

I am reminded of an old Chinese Rule of Health:

On one day in the week, if possible, neither read nor write poetry.

Hugo Vickers has sent me a copy of a letter, addressed to a school health visitor, which he found among the papers of his aunt, the late Baroness Vickers DBE:

Dear Miss The Nurse,

You scent our Harry oame bicause eh smealt e smeals the same as is farther I ave slept with him twenty yrs, e sutes me and eel ave to sute you and you must be an ole made wot doessent no the smeal of er man.

Yours

With love Mrs Swift

The things she knew, let her forget again –
   The voices in the sky, the fear, the cold,
The gaping shepherds, and the queer old men
   Piling their clumsy gifts of foreign gold.

Let her have laughter with her little one;
   Teach her the endless, tuneless songs to sing;
Grant her the right to whisper to her son
   The foolish names one dare not call a King.

Keep from her dreams the rumble of a crowd,
   The smell of rough-cut wood, the trail of red,
The thick and chilly whiteness of the shroud
   That wraps the strange new body of the dead.

Ah, let her go, kind Lord, where mothers go
   And boast his pretty words and ways, and plan
The proud and happy years that they shall know
   Together, when her son is grown a man.

Dorothy Parker

Some years ago I was contacted by Tony Graham, an Australian engineer and keen industrial conservationist, who had bought the remains of Somerset's last ironworks and a beautiful wooded gorge near the village of Mells. He planned to convert a handsome but decaying office building into a house. But no sooner had he bought the property than serious bureaucratic bodies converged on him.

Bat experts found a colony of greater horseshoe bats in his roof, and had the building declared a Site of Special Scientific Interest, ruling that the bats could not be disturbed – but the Victorian Society then had the building listed, demanding that it be fully restored.

Industrial archaeologists became so excited by the overgrown foundry ruins that they had them declared a Historic Monument, demanding that all vegetation be cleared from the site as soon as possible. Almost immediately other naturalists discovered rare ferns growing on the same ruins and insisted that the vegetation should on no account be touched.

Beset by all these incompatible demands, Mr Graham called a site meeting, including local council officials, telling them that if only they could work out what it was they wanted him to conserve, he would cheerfully comply.

The resulting discussion, which I attended, was surreal. One highlight was a fierce argument between the chief bat lady and the Victorian Society as to whether, if Mr Graham was allowed to build a bathroom at the back of the house, the bats might not be disturbed by light from its window as they flew in and out of their roost. When it was suggested that this might be remedied by a blind over the bathroom window, the bat lady indignantly pointed out that Mr Graham might forget to pull his blind. When Mr Graham suggested the installation of a light sensor so that the blind would close automatically, the Victorian Society objected that this would be out of keeping with a listed building.

The impasse thus continued for months, until one Sunday two village boys got wet in the stream in front of the building and went in to light a fire to dry their clothes. The result: the building burned down and the bats happily decamped to a nearby tunnel.

Thanks to the best efforts of all those wild-eyed conservationists, Mr Graham was left with nothing but a gutted and batless ruin.

However real the person,
However real the bed,
For making love in darkness
Little can be said
That can't be said for some bright dream
Inside a sleeping head.

Anon. (ninth-century Japanese),
translated by Graeme Wilson

His Highness Prince Johannes von Thurn und Taxis, who has died aged
sixty-four, was an aristocrat whose tastes sometimes appeared more
questionable than his antecedents.

He was also a successful business man, who more than recouped the
family fortune after the loss of six castles and some 200,000 acres in the
wake of the Second World War. The Thurn und Taxis family originated
in Lombardy and rose to prominence some four hundred years ago
when they carried letters all over the Austrian Empire, acquiring the
title of Hereditary Grand Postmaster General of the Empire in 1595 and,
a century later, the rank of Prince . . .

The feudal grandeur which the Prince maintained at his 500-room
palace – Schloss St Emmeram, a former monastery on the Danube at
Regensburg in Bavaria – would have done credit to any of his ancestors.
To the end, the Schloss was staffed by servants in livery and powdered
wigs. Five chefs ministered to the caprices of the palate, and a clock-
maker was employed full-time to wind and service the various time-
pieces. In winter there were boar hunts, with beaters in red and blue
tabards driving the prey through the forest; and the day would end
with gamekeepers honouring the slaughtered beasts with ritual salu-
tations upon the horn.

Prince Johannes believed that aristocrats were different from ordinary
mortals, and his own behaviour supported this notion. A tall, commanding figure, with the look of an owl and a slow, ceremonial style of
speech, he gave the impression that his features had been pickled by
years of good living. His entourage spoke of him as an intelligent,
intensely observant man, with a lively sense of humour and an almost
psychic awareness of the foibles of those he met. More dispassionate
observers noted his outspoken comments on Jews and negroes.

As to the Prince's humour, no doubt it went down well in Germany.
In 1971 on his way to the Shah of Iran's extravagant celebrations in
Persepolis, he secreted some coleslaw in a sickbag on the aircraft; during
the flight he feigned sickness, retched violently and proceeded, to the
disgust of his unaristocratic fellow passengers, to eat the contents of the
sickbag.

Prince Johannes's family had featured on both sides in the Second
World War, and he never lost an opportunity of teasing his 'bad
German' relations, in whose presence he would finger the lampshades
and wonder at the consistency of the fabric.

As a bachelor, the Prince was constantly photographed with the world's most glamorous women. He indulged his reputation as an international playboy to the hilt until, in his fifties, he married Gloria von Schonburg-Glauclau, a vivacious 22-year-old German countess given to dyeing her hair various colours, to riding a powerful motor-bicycle around the German countryside, and to singing at parties. It was an unconventional marriage. The Princess would throw her arms exuberantly around her husband's neck and declare: '*Oh Johannes. Ich liebe dich!* I love you! I want to cut your throat and drink your blood!'

When Prince Johannes celebrated his sixtieth birthday in 1986, Princess Gloria arranged for the cake to be adorned with sixty chocolate candles sculpted in the form of the male member. The Prince, though, was embarrassed that this tribute to his virility should be paraded before his tenantry, whose children eagerly fell upon the illuminating trophies . . .

He never could decide what to write
About, knowing only that his pen
Must not rust in the stale tears of men
Too long dead, nor yet take to flight
Before measuring the thought's height
Above the earth, whose green thoroughfares
Though hedged thickly with the heart's cares,
Still let in the sun's natural light.

He tried truth; but the pen's scalpel tip
Was too sharp; thinly the blood ran
From unseen wounds, but too red to dip
Again in, so, back where he began,
He tried love; slowly the blood congealed
Like dark flowers saddening a field.

R. S. Thomas

History is littered with wars which everybody said would never happen.

Enoch Powell

In March 1815, Napoleon Bonaparte escaped from Elba and marched on Paris. The French Government newspaper, Le Moniteur Universel, *gave a brief daily report on his progress. Here are some examples:*

L'anthropophage est sorti de son repaire.

L'ogre de Corse vient de débarquer au Golfe Juan.

Le tigre est arrivé a Gap.

Le monstre a couché à Grenoble.

Le tyran a traversé Lyon.

L'usurpateur a été vu à soixante lieues de la capitale.

Bonaparte s'avance à grands pas, mais il n'entrera jamais dans Paris.

Napoléon sera demain sous nos remparts.

L'Empereur est arrive à Fontainebleau.

Sa Majesté Impériale et Royale a fait hier au soir son entrée dans son château des Tuileries au milieu de ses fidèles sujets.

A riddle – not by Byron as used to be thought, but by Catherine Maria Fanshawe:

'Twas whispered in heaven, 'twas muttered in hell,
And echo caught faintly the sound as it fell;
On the confines of earth 'twas permitted to rest,
And the depth of the ocean its presence confessed.
'Twill be found in the sphere when 'tis riven asunder,
Be seen in the lightning, and heard in the thunder.
'Twas allotted to man with his earliest breath,
Attends at his birth and awaits him in death;
Presides o'er his happiness, honour and health,
Is the prop of his house, and the end of his wealth.
In the heaps of the miser 'tis hoarded with care,
But is sure to be lost on his prodigal heir.
It begins every hope, every wish it must bound,
With the husbandman toils, and with monarchs is crowned;
Without it the soldier, the seaman may roam,
But woe to the wench who expels it from home!
In the whispers of conscience its voice will be found,
Nor e'en in the whirlwind of passion is drowned.
'Twill not soften the heart; and tho' deaf to the ear,
It will make it acutely and instantly hear;
Yet in shade let it rest like a delicate flower,
Ah! breathe on it softly – it dies in an hour.

[*The answer is at the foot of page 339.*]

Two pieces on the pleasures of bathing. The first comes from a letter from William Allingham, author of The Fairies *('Up the airy mountain, down the rushy glen') and of the most enjoyable of Victorian diaries, frequently quoted in former* Crackers – *to his friend Alexander Munro:*

I bathed this morning in the sea, in a gully of a reef on which the breakers were rolling in magnificently, walls of dark water advancing till they toppled over at one end and the brilliant foam ran along the line like fire along a battery. I had left off bathing for years, and now find it a glorious addition to my enjoyments. It ought to be bracing for mind as well as body, for it often requires some resolution to make the move which abandons terra firma and tailors at one stride, and plunges one into the cold mysterious kingdom of fishes and drowned men . . .

The second is from the far better-known diary of the Reverend Francis Kilvert, for Friday 12 June 1874:

This morning a rough and troublesome sea came tumbling into the bay and plunging in foam upon the shore. The bay was full of white horses. At Shanklin one has to adopt the detestable custom of bathing in drawers. If ladies don't like to see men naked why don't they keep away from the sight? Today I had a pair of drawers given me which I could not keep on. The rough waves stripped them off and tore them down round my ancles [sic]. While thus fettered I was seized and flung down by a heavy sea which retreating suddenly left me lying naked on the sharp shingle, from which I rose streaming with blood. After this I took the wretched and dangerous rag off, and of course there were some ladies looking on as I came up out of the water.

From an unpublished letter by the English art critic Matthew Prichard to his friend, Mrs Isabella Stewart Gardner:

Monte Carlo
March 24, 1914

In the English church at Monte Carlo it is impossible to give out a hymn with a number as low as 36, for fear lest the whole congregation leave the edifice to play the figure at the tables.

'The mysterious and mystic Prichard' – as Mrs Gardner once described him – was at the time Deputy Director of the Boston Museum of Fine Arts. He had been warmly championed by Bernard Berenson for the Directorship in 1906 – alas, in vain.

Seventy is wormwood,
Seventy is gall,
But it's better to be seventy
Than not alive at all.

So wrote Phyllis McGinley on her seventieth birthday. But Thornton Wilder, on his, was a good deal more up-beat:

I was an old man when I was twelve; and now I *am* an old man, *and it's splendid.*

Bonus

This hitherto unknown letter from Lady Macbeth to Lady Macduff was discovered by Maurice Baring and published in his Dead Letters *of 1910:*

Most Private

> The Palace, Forres
> October 10

My dearest Flora,

I am sending this letter by Ross, who is starting for Fife tomorrow morning. I wonder if you could possibly come here for a few days. You would bring Jeamie of course. Macbeth is devoted to children. I think we could make you quite comfortable, although of course palaces are never very comfortable, and it's all so different from dear Inverness. And there is the tiresome Court etiquette and the people, especially the Heads of the Clans, who are so touchy and insist on one's observing every tradition. For instance, the bagpipes begin in the early morning; the pipers walk round the castle a little after sunrise, and this I find very trying, as you know what a bad sleeper I am. Only two nights ago I nearly fell out of the window walking in my sleep. The doctor, who I must say is a charming man (he was the late King's doctor and King Duncan always used to say he was the only man who really understood his constitution) is giving me mandragora mixed with poppy and syrup; but so far it has not done me any good; but then I always was a wretched sleeper and now I am worse, because – well, I am coming at last to what I really want to say.

I am in very great trouble and I beg you to come here if you can, because you would be the greatest help. You shall have a bedroom facing south, and Jeamie shall be next to you, and my maid can look after you both, and as Macduff is going to England I think it would really be wiser and *safer* for you to come here than to stay all alone in that lonely castle of yours in these troublesome times, when there are so many robbers about and one never knows what may not happen.

I confess I have been very much put about lately. (You quite understand if you come we shall have plenty of opportunities of seeing each other alone in spite of all the tiresome etiquette and ceremonies, and of course you must treat me just the same as before; only in *public* you must just throw in a 'Majesty' now and then and curtsey and call me 'Ma'am' so as not to shock the people.) I am sorry to say Macbeth is not at all in good case. He is really not at all well, and the fact is he has never got over the terrible tragedy that happened at Inverness. At first I thought it was quite natural he should be upset. Of course very few people know how fond he was of his cousin. King Duncan was his favourite cousin. They had travelled together in England, and they were much more like brothers than cousins, although the King was so much older than he is. I shall never forget the evening when the King arrived after the battle against those horrid Norwegians. I was very nervous as it was, after having gone through all the anxiety of knowing that Macbeth was in danger. Then on top of that, just after I heard that he was alive and well, the messenger arrived telling me that the King was on his way to Inverness. Of course I had got nothing ready, and Elspeth our housekeeper put on a face as much as to say that we could not possibly manage in the time. However, I said she *must* manage. I knew our cousin wouldn't expect too much, and I spent the whole day making those flat scones he used to be so fond of.

I was already worried then because Macbeth, who is superstitious, said he had met three witches on the way (he said something about it in his letter) and they had apparently been uncivil to him. I thought they were gypsies and that he had not crossed their palm with silver, but when he arrived he was still brooding over this, and was quite *odd* in his way of speaking about it. I didn't think much of this at the time, as I put it down to the strain of what he had gone through, and the reaction which must always be great after such a time; but now it all comes back to me, and now that I think over it in view of what has happened since, I cannot help owning to myself that he was not himself, and if I had not known what a sober man he was, I should almost have thought the 1030 (Hildebrand) whisky had gone to his head – because when he talked of the old women he was quite incoherent: just like a man who has had an hallucination. But I did not think of all this till afterwards, as I put it down to the strain, as I have just told you.

But now! Well, I must go back a little way so as to make everything clear to you. Duncan arrived, and nothing could be more civil than he was. He went out of his way to be nice to everybody and praised the castle, the situation, the view, and even the birds' nests on the walls! (All this, of course, went straight to my heart.) Donalbain and Malcolm were with him. They, I thought at the time, were not at all well brought up. They had not got their father's manners, and they talked in a loud voice and gave themselves airs.

Duncan had supper by himself, and before he went to bed he sent me a most beautiful diamond ring, which I shall always wear. Then we all went to bed. Macbeth was not himself that evening, and he frightened me out of my wits by talking of ghosts and witches and daggers. I did not, however, think anything serious was the matter and I still put it down to the strain and the excitement. However, I took the precaution of pouring a drop or two of my sleeping draught into the glass of water which he always drinks before going to bed, so that at least he might have a good night's rest. I suppose I did not give him a strong enough dose. (But one cannot be too careful with drugs, especially mandragora, which is bad for the heart.) At any rate, whether it was that or the awful weather we had that night (nearly all the trees in the park were blown down, and it will never be quite the same again) or whether it was that the hall porter got tipsy (why they choose the one day in the year to drink when one has guests, and it really matters, I never could understand!) and made the most dreadful noise and used really disgraceful language at the front door about five o'clock in the morning, I don't know. At any rate, we were all disturbed long before I had meant that we should be called (breakfast wasn't nearly ready and Elspeth was only just raking out the fires). But, as I say, we were all woken up, and Macduff went to call the King, and came back with the terrible news.

Macbeth turned quite white, and at first my only thought was for him. I thought he was going to have a stroke or a fit. You know he has a very nervous, high-strung constitution, and nothing could be worse for him than a shock like this. I confess that I myself felt as though I wished the earth would open and swallow me up. To think of such a thing happening in our house!

Banquo, too, was white as a sheet; but the only people who behaved badly (of course this is strictly between ourselves, and I do implore you not to repeat it, as it would really do harm if it got about that I had said this, but you are safe, aren't you, Flora?) were Donalbain and Malcolm. Donalbain said nothing at all, and all Malcolm said when he was told that his father had been murdered was: 'Oh! By whom?' I could not understand how he could behave in such a heartless way before so many people; but I must say in fairness that all the Duncans have a very odd way of showing grief.

Of course the first thing I thought was 'Who can have done it?'

and I suppose in a way it will always remain a mystery. There is no doubt that the chamber grooms actually did the deed; but whether they had any accomplices, whether it was just the act of drunkards (it turned out that the whole household had been drinking that night and not only the hall porter) or whether they were *instigated* by anyone else (of course don't quote me as having suggested such a thing) we shall never know. Much as I dislike Malcolm and Donalbain, and shocking as I think their behaviour has been, and not only shocking but *suspicious*, I should not like anyone to think that I suspected them of so awful a crime. It is one thing to be bad-mannered, it is another to be a parricide. However, there is no getting over the fact that by their conduct, by their extraordinary behaviour and flight to England, they made people suspect them.

I have only just now come to the real subject of my letter. At first Macbeth bore up pretty well in spite of the blow, the shock, and the extra worry of the coronation following immediately on all this; but no sooner had we settled down at Forres than I soon saw he was far from being himself.

His appetite was bad; he slept badly, and was cross to the servants, making scenes about nothing. When I tried to ask him about his health he lost his temper. At last one day it all came out and I realized that another tragedy was in store for us. Macbeth is suffering from hallucinations; this whole terrible business has unhinged his mind. The doctor always said he was highly strung, and the fact is he has had another attack, or whatever it is, the same as he had after the battle, when he thought he had seen three witches. (I afterwards found out from Banquo, who was with him at the time, that the matter was even worse than I suspected.) He is suffering from a terrible delusion. He thinks (of course you will never breathe this to a soul) that he killed Duncan! You can imagine what I am going through. Fortunately, nobody has noticed it.

Only last night another calamity happened. Banquo had a fall out riding and was killed. That night we had a banquet we could not possibly put off. On purpose I gave strict orders that Macbeth was not to be told of the accident until the banquet was over, but Lennox (who has no more discretion than a parrot) told him, and in the middle of dinner he had another attack, and I had only just time to get everyone to go away before he began to rave. As it was, it must have been noticed that he wasn't himself.

I am in a terrible position. I never know when these fits are coming on, and I am afraid of people talking, because if it once gets about, people are so spiteful that somebody is sure to start the rumour that it's true. Imagine our position, then! So I beg you, dear Flora, to keep all this to yourself, and if possible to come here as soon as possible.

I am, your affectionate

HARRIET R.

PS Don't forget to bring Jeamie. It will do Macbeth good to see a child in the house.

[The answer to the riddle on p. 331 is the letter H.]

Acknowledgements

The author and publishers are grateful to the following for permission to quote copyright material.

Faber & Faber Ltd for 'Musée des Beaux Arts' from *Collected Shorter Poems, 1927–1957* by W. H. Auden (Faber, 1969), © W. H. Auden, 1966; The Random House Archive & Library for 'What does this sudden uneasiness mean', translated by J. Mavrogordato, from *Poems* by C. P. Cavafy (Chatto & Windus, 1971); Constable & Robinson Publishing for extracts from *Library Looking Glass: A Personal Anthology* (Constable, 1975) and *The Cecils of Hatfield House* (Constable, 1973), both by Lord David Cecil; the Paul Dehn Estate, London Management Ltd for 'Alternative Endings to an Unwritten Ballad' by Paul Dehn from *The Oxford Book of Comic Verse*, edited by John Gross (Oxford University Press, 1994); the author for 'On his Blackberries Gone Mouldy' from *Collected Poems 1949–1984* by Maureen Duffy (Hamish Hamilton, 1985); Ecclesiastes, xxi, 1–7 from *The Authorized Version of the Bible (The King James Bible)*, the rights in which are vested in the Crown, are reproduced by permission of the Crown's Patentee, Cambridge University Press; Mrs Margo Ewart for 'A remarkable thing about wine' from *Collected Poems, 1980–1990* by Gavin Ewart (Hutchinson, 1991); John Murray (Publishers) for extracts from *Mani* by Patrick Leigh Fermor (Murray, 1958); The Random House Archive & Library on behalf of the Estate of Robert Frost for 'Forgive, O Lord, my little jokes on Thee' by Robert Frost from *The Poetry of Robert Frost*, edited by Edward Connery Lathem (Jonathan Cape); Carcanet Press for 'The difference between you and her' by Robert Graves from *Complete Poems*, 3 volumes (Carcanet, 1995–99); David Higham Associates for a letter from Edward Marsh to Christopher Hassall from *Edward Marsh* by Christopher Hassall (Longman, 1959); Faber & Faber Ltd for 'Blackberry-Picking' from *New Selected Poems, 1966–1987* by Seamus Heaney (Faber, 1990); The Society of Authors as the Literary Representative of the Estate of A. E. Housman for 'Hallelujah! was the only observation' from *Collected Poems and Selected Prose* by A. E. Housman (Penguin Twentieth-Century Classics, 1989); Lawrence James for the extract on Sir Bulwark Bloode; Duff Hart-Davis for extracts by Sir Rupert Hart-Davis from *The Lyttelton – Hart-Davis Letters: Volume 4* (Murray, 1982); A. M. Heath & Company Ltd for an extract from *Venice Observed* by Mary McCarthy (Penguin, 1985), © The Estate of Mary McCarthy; J. J.

Dallyn for 'Dusting' from *Verses* by Viola Meynell (Martin Secker, 1919); Elizabeth Barnett, literary executor, for 'What my lips have kissed' and Sonnet XXX of *Fatal Interview* by Edna St Vincent Millay, from *Collected Poems* (HarperCollins Publishers), © 1923, 1930, 1951, 1958 by Edna St Vincent Millay and Norma Millay Ellis; Duckworth & Company for 'One Perfect Rose' and 'Prayer for a New Mother' from *The Collected Dorothy Parker* (Duckworth, 1973); Constable & Robinson Publishing for 'The Old Lute' by Po Chu-I, translated by Arthur Waley; from *170 Chinese Poems* (Constable, 1987); David Prior for a letter to *The Times* (25 June 1992); Sir Ian Rankin for Sir Hugh Rankin's entry in *Who's Who* (A. & C. Black, 1987); The Society of Authors, on behalf of the Bernard Shaw Estate, for an extract from 'Form and Design in Music' by George Bernard Shaw from *The World* (31 May 1893); National Poetry Foundation Publications for 'The Bramble Route' from *Thinning Grapes* by Mary Sheepshanks (National Poetry Foundation, 1982); David Higham Associates for an extract from *Left Hand, Right Hand!* by Osbert Sitwell (Macmillan, 1944); John Murray (Publishers) for an extract from *Traveller's Prelude* by Freya Stark (Murray, 1950); Sadie Williams for 'Heaven' from *The Collected Poems of A. S. J. Tessimond* (Whiteknights Press, 1985); A. P. Watt Ltd on behalf of The Royal Literary Fund for 'The Last Hero' from *Collected Poems* by G. K. Chesterton (Methuen, 1933); A. P. Watt Ltd on behalf of The National Trust for Places of Historic Interest or Natural Beauty for 'How far is St Helena from a little child at play?' by Rudyard Kipling from *Other Men's Flowers*, edited by Archibald Percival Wavell (Cape, 1944); Estate of John Wells c/o Rogers, Coleridge & White Ltd., 20 Powis Mews, London WII IJN for the Obituary of Sylvia Chancellor from *The Times* (29 October 1996), © John Wells 1996; Sister Philippa Edwards on behalf of Miss Mollie Martin for 'My Lord is gone away to serve the King' (Anon.) from *Lyrics from the Chinese*, edited/translated by Helen Waddell (Malvern Publishing, 1987); The Random House Archive & Library for an extract from *Bauhaus to Our House* by Tom Wolfe (Picador, 1993); The Random House Archive & Library for an extract from the diary of Virginia Woolf (31 August 1928), from *Diary. Volume 3: 1925–30*, edited by A. O. Bell (Penguin Books, 1982).

The publishers would be pleased to rectify any omissions brought to their notice at the earliest opportunity.

Index

Authors of substantive items are listed in CAPITALS